THE
END
OF THE
EURO

Praise for Johan Van Overtveldt's *Bernanke's Test*

"Though a phrase like 'the drama of the central banker' might once have drawn snickers, today the chairman of the Federal Reserve has become something of a star. This contemporary history, from the 1970s chairmanship of Paul Volcker on, provides an excellent introduction to the current financial crisis.... It's early for predictions, but Van Overtveldt portrays Bernanke as the man for the season: an academic focused on the Great Depression, Bernanke became a member of the Fed's Board of Governors in 2002. Though conventional, Bernanke's present approach—further cutting the federal funds rate to spur liquidity, keeping his hands off interest rates—and belief in regulation, set him apart from Greenspan, while his commitment to transparency and clear communication align him with the new administration. Anyone who wants to understand the role of the Fed in the current crisis will find this an accessible primer."   —*Publishers Weekly*

"Should we feel better that the chairman of the Federal Reserve is an authority on the Great Depression? Perhaps so, suggests Belgium-based economist Van Overtveldt.... Van Overtveldt is particularly clear when he examines pronouncements on the part of both Bernanke and Greenspan that he considers 'spectacularly wrong.' A timely study that will help readers interpret the headlines."   —*Kirkus Reviews*

"Here at last is a book about the U.S. Federal Reserve that is neither impossibly technical nor populist. The author is obviously extremely familiar with the American financial and political scene. But, perhaps because he is resident in Belgium, he avoids the twin sins of U.S.-type blockbusters of excessive length and arch chapter headings and introductions such as: 'While Joe Smith was trimming his lawn the telephone rang ... it was the White House.'"   —Samuel Brittan, *Financial Times*

Praise for *The Chicago School*

"Far more than a trot through the dry record of academic papers. Recollections, in interviews with the author or from published sources, illuminate personalities, rows and controversy.... This is an admirably detailed and thoroughly welcome history of a great centre of economic thought."   —*The Economist*

"A landmark in the history of economic thought."   —Tyler Cowen

THE
END
OF THE
EURO

The uneasy future of the European Union

JOHAN VAN OVERTVELDT

AN AGATE IMPRINT

CHICAGO

Printed in the United States of America.

Library of Congress Cataloging-in-Publication Data

Overtveldt, Johan van.

The end of the euro : the uneasy future of the European Union / Johan Van Overtveldt.

p. cm.

Includes bibliographical references and index.

ISBN-13: 978-1-932841-61-9 (hard cover : alk. paper)

ISBN-10: 1-932841-61-X (hard cover : alk. paper)

ISBN-13: 978-1-57284-688-3 (ebook : alk. paper)

ISBN-10: 1-57284-688-7 (ebook : alk. paper)

1. Euro. 2. European currency unit. 3. Currency question--European Union countries. 4. European Union countries--Economic policy. 5. Monetary policy--European Union countries. I. Title.

HG925.M854 2008

332.4'94--dc23

2011034982

10 9 8 7 6 5 4 3 2 1   15 14 13 12 11

B2 Books is an imprint of Agate Publishing.

Agate books are available in bulk at discount prices. For more information, go to agatepublishing.com.

NOTHING IS POSSIBLE WITHOUT MEN AND WOMEN, BUT NOTHING IS LASTING WITHOUT INSTITUTIONS.

—Jean Monnet, founding father of European Unity

WHAT WENT WRONG WASN'T WHAT HAPPENED THIS YEAR. WHAT WENT WRONG WAS WHAT HAPPENED IN THE FIRST ELEVEN YEARS OF THE EURO'S HISTORY.... IT WAS LIKE SOME KIND OF SLEEPING PILL, SOME KIND OF DRUG. WE WEREN'T AWARE OF THE UNDERLYING PROBLEMS.

—Herman Van Rompuy, president of the European Union

IN A WORLD OF SOVEREIGN STATES...NOTHING CAN BE REGARDED AS TRULY IRREVERSIBLE.

—Benjamin Cohen, professor of international political economy at the University of California, Santa Barbara

THE CURRENCY UNION IS OUR COMMON DESTINY. IT IS A QUESTION, NO MORE OR LESS, OF THE PRESERVATION OF THE EUROPEAN IDEA. THAT IS OUR HISTORICAL TASK: FOR IF THE EURO FAILS, THEN EUROPE FAILS.

—Angela Merkel, German chancellor

THE EUROPEAN SINGLE CURRENCY IS BOUND TO FAIL, ECONOMICALLY, POLITICALLY, AND INDEED SOCIALLY, THOUGH THE TIMING, OCCASION, AND FULL CONSEQUENCES ARE ALL NECESSARILY STILL UNCLEAR.

—Margaret Thatcher, British Prime Minister, 1979–1990

THERE IS NO CRISIS OF THE EURO.

—Jean-Claude Trichet, president of the European Central Bank

IT IS PREPOSTEROUS FOR EUROPEAN POLITICIANS TO CLAIM THAT THE WHOLE CRISIS IS BEING CAUSED BY IRRATIONAL MARKETS.

—Kenneth Rogoff, Harvard professor and former chief economist of the International Monetary Fund

Table of Contents

Foreword

JOHAN VAN OVERTVELDT'S SHORT BOOK ABOUT THE
euro is most timely because of the financial crisis in Greece,
Spain, Portugal, and Ireland—and the extensive deliberations
in national capitals about sustaining the euro. The narrative is both
comprehensive and punchy. The first chapter focuses on history,
laying out the political forces (especially in France) that led to efforts at reducing nationalist barriers within Europe to the movement of goods, services, and human talent among countries. The
second chapter is analytical, asking whether the major countries
in Europe would together pass the criteria for an optimum currency area. The third chapter focuses on the financial crisis that has
rocked the eurozone since 2009, and the fourth and final chapter is the author's judgment that Germany will leave the euro
because the financial costs of continued adherence are too high.

The European Union is a work in progress, and the adoption
of the euro was one more step in writing its constitution. Constitutions define rights, privileges, obligations, and commitments, and
provide the rules and procedures for amending the statements on
rights and obligations. Actions and decisions become precedents
which then are attached to the constitution, although with lesser
legal standing than the articles.

The U.S. Constitution was written in a few weeks over the summer of 1776, when the thirteen colonies were about to declare their
independence from Britain, the mother country. A war was immi-

nent because King George III would not accept the unilateral action of the colonists. The initiative to write a constitution reflected that the prior contract, the Articles of Confederation, did not provide for a sufficiently strong central authority when the colonies were about to be involved in a war. Four or five individuals from each of the thirteen colonies participated in the drafting the constitution. Four million people then lived in the thirteen colonies; they shared a language, a culture, and a modest history—but there were commercial rivalries among the colonies and between the agricultural interests in some states and the mercantile interests in Pennsylvania and New York. The agricultural states wanted a less powerful central authority.

Developing the constitution for the new Europe is much more complex and involves a series of treaties over more than fifty years. These treaties were sometimes named after the city where the treaty was established and sometimes after an individual. Van Overtveldt provides a succinct and comprehensive history of this development The first treaty established the Coal and Steel Community, which involved six countries. Now the Union involves twenty-six countries and more than three hundred million people. Their cultural histories differ and they have had many many wars and territorial and other disputes. The larger participating countries have ten to twenty times the population and economic clout of the smaller ones. The process of building the new Europe is very pragmatic—very Anglo-Saxon.

The new Europe faces the same problem that preoccupied those in Philadelphia, which was how much power to allocate to the central authority. The metaphor can be illustrated by the contrast between the patterns of railroad tracks in France and in Germany. The tracks in the French railroad system radiate primarily from Paris while those in German systems radiate from the regional centers including Hamburg, Munich, Leipzig, and even Berlin. The French and the smaller countries that are members of the European Union want a strong central authority, while the Germans and the British want a much weaker one. The Germans recognize that a strong central authority would constrain their own choices and involve a larger transfer of money from Berlin to Brussels.

The new Europe has been a grand success. There were three major wars between France and Germany, along with many other participants, between 1870 and 1940. Europe has been at peace since the 1940s, with the exception of the wars associated with the disintegration of Yugoslavia and the turmoil in Cyprus, and the war over cod and protected fishing rights between Britain and Iceland. Europe has become amazingly prosperous.

The innovation of the 1990s was that Europe began to develop along two tracks: an inner club that included most of the countries in the European Union who chose to adopt a common currency and an outer club who did not. Britain and several smaller countries decided not to join the inner club. The two-club track is another example of pragmatism.

Skepticism about whether the euro will survive is based on the inability to deal with the "Greek problem." Greece and Portugal incurred large fiscal deficits because "the money was there"—they were like banana republics that would borrow as much as they could. The government of Greece had engaged in hanky panky when it applied for membership in the European Monetary Union; it satisfied the Maastricht criteria only because it had massaged the data on its deficit and on its indebtedness. Moreover, Greece joined the euro at the "wrong exchange rate"; its massive fiscal deficit has resulted primarily from its large trade deficit that in turn reflected that its costs and prices were too high. Many of the major European banks were the willing participants in the financial folly: Greece and Portugal could not have incurred these deficits if the money had not been there to finance them. Both Greece and Portugal had primary fiscal deficits; all of the money to pay the interest on their indebtedness came from new loans.

Then, at one stage, the banks that financed the Greek deficit recognized that Greece was overextended and said, "No new money." Because the primary deficit was six or seven percent of GDP, Greece would not have enough money to pay the interest to the bank lenders and meet the government payroll. Hence, the Greek government would default and it would still have to reduce its domestic payments to government employees and vendors by 5 or 6 percent. Default probably would mean that Greece would have to leave the inner club.

Then the lenders and investors recognized that some of the other governments including Ireland and Spain also had primary fiscal deficits. The financial situations of these countries differed from those of Greece and Portugal; both Ireland and Spain developed large fiscal deficits after the implosion of their real estate bubbles. Both are vibrant exporters.

What were the policy options for Germany, France, and the other European governments with stable finances? One was to provide government loans to the governments of Greece, Portugal, and Ireland to enable them to finance their deficits until they had declined to a sustainable value; this choice has involved setting targets and conditions for the performance of the government of Greece in reducing its fiscal deficit. A second was to facilitate a default that would reduce the indebtedness of these governments to 50 or 60 percent of GDP. A third was to provide financial assistance to the banks, and let the banks work out their problems with the governments of Greece and Portugal. A fourth was for Greece to separate from the monetary union, which would have involved the development of a new currency for Greece, an effective devaluation, and probably a default. A fifth option is that Germany leaves the euro.

There has been an immense amount of hostage taking—implicit threats that if the money is not forthcoming, something bad will happen. The European banks are using the governments of Greece and the other heavily indebted countries to obtain a bailout of their misbegotten loans. These governments are threatening the solvency of the banks as a way of getting more financial support.

The immediate problem is how to get through this crisis. The banks need to be recapitalized, perhaps along the lines of the Troubled Asset Relief Program (TARP). Governments should acquire equity ownership interests in the banks that decide to ask for financial support. Lines need to drawn, not in sand, but in hard concrete; the message to the heavily indebted countries should be "This is the total amount of money that will be available—no more. When the money runs out, you're on your own. If you feel you must leave the inner club, either temporarily or permanently, well, that's your choice. Recognize that we are much more important to you than you are to us."

The longer-run problem is to ensure that problems of this type do not occur again, and the moral hazard issue of ensuring that the inevitable bailouts at this time do not increase the likelihood of free-riding behavior in the future. Two factors complicate the resolution of the problem. One is the fiction that each country is sovereign; debtors and especially small ones are never in the same position as large countries. The second is the unwillingness to contemplate the unthinkable that one or several countries might leave the inner club.

This scenario differs from van Overtveldt's that Germany will take the initiative and opt out. If Greece takes the initiative and leaves, the euro appreciates. At the technical level, it is much more difficult to write the scenario that would involve Germany leaving the euro than it is to write the scenario that would have Greece leaving the euro. Still, if Germany takes the initiative and leaves, the new super mark also appreciates, and by a much larger amount than if Greece leaves. Germany then would be committing economic suicide. That seems unlikely, but it might occur. Germany has committed suicide before. Hence, it seems more likely that Germany will set the conditions so that the smaller countries decide to opt out because the costs of remaining in the inner club are too high.

One question posed by the crisis in Greece is whether a monetary union requires a fiscal union—or perhaps how much of a fiscal union is required to backstop the monetary union. The long-run problem is to ensure that imbalances in payments among member countries are self-limiting. A common monetary policy suggests that the inflation rate will not differ significantly. But productivity in the countries with large manufacturing sectors will be higher than in the other member countries. The preferred means of adjustment is that wages increase more rapidly in the countries with the more rapid productivity gains.

Van Overtveldt's book does a masterful job of ranking the issues and identifying the measures that must be adopted if the grand exercise in writing a constitution for Europe is to succeed. The ratio of the value of the book to the number of pages is very high.

—*Robert Z. Aliber*

Robert Z. Aliber is professor emeritus of international economics and finance at the University of Chicago Booth School of Business. He is director of the Center for Studies in International Finance; on the research staff for the Committee for Economic Development and Commission on Money and Credit; and senior economic advisor for the Agency for Economic Development, U.S. Department of State.

Introduction

THE EURO IS STRUGGLING TO SURVIVE. FOR MORE than a decade, political decision makers have ignored economists' warnings about the European monetary union's structural shortcomings. Today, Greece, Ireland, and Portugal are suffering acute financial crises, with Spain, Italy and Belgium coming close to going down the same path. The general atmosphere in the European Union (EU) is filled with uncertainty and fear for the future. The euro member states must change the rules of the game if the union is to survive, but Europe's political leaders have failed to act decisively.

Financial markets "do no not understand the euro," claimed Wolfgang Schäuble, Germany's minister of finance, in early December 2010.[1] Christine Lagarde, who was at the time the finance minister of France and is now head of the International Monetary Fund, remarked in a radio interview a few days earlier, "Europe is difficult to understand for the markets."[2]

At the time the crisis in the eurozone broke out, late 2009, the authorities simply denied it. It was not a crisis at all, they claimed. It was simply a run of bad luck that would go away as quickly as it had come. Within weeks, of course, the intensity of the crisis destroyed any credence this claim may have had, and European officials adopted a new stance: The crisis was caused by greed, speculators, and irresponsible and irrational behavior in the financial markets. Germany led the charge as many officials added a third argument, pointing to irresponsible policies that existed in Greece and Ireland, among other countries.

European leaders most often blamed greedy speculators and irresponsible markets, especially during the early months of the sovereign debt crisis. There was one notable exception—Austrian Minister of Finance Josef Proell, who declared in the spring of 2010 that he was "against putting all the blame on speculation. Speculation is only successful against countries that have mismanaged their finances for years."[3]

Several, including German Chancellor Angela Merkel, French President Nicolas Sarkozy, EU President Herman Van Rompuy, and European Commission President José Manuel Barroso, explicitly blamed hedge funds, wealthy private speculators, rating agencies, bond market vigilantes, and investment banks (or what was left of them). Nothing was fundamentally wrong with the euro's health, they all claimed. Anders Borg, Sweden's minister of finance, crucified "Anglo-Saxon financial capitalism and markets" by comparing them to a "pack of wolves" hunting savagely in a rabid effort to "tear the weaker countries apart."[4] Jean-Claude Juncker, the prime minister of Luxembourg and president of the eurogroup of finance ministers, even suggested that an organized worldwide attack on the euro might be afoot. All around Europe, leaders insisted that the solution was simple: restoring the primacy of politics over speculative finance.

Simon Tilford, chief economist at the London-based Centre for European Reform, pointed out that "to suggest that the markets are partly to blame for the crisis or for prolonging it only serves to reinforce the perception of European other-worldliness. The markets have simply called the EU's bluff. Indeed, they should have done so earlier—that way the crisis might have been avoided."[5] Wolfgang

Münchau, commentator for the *Financial Times*, argued that "Europe's leaders are not solving the problem. They are fighting a public relations war... We know from the history of European financial crises that politicians are ill-equipped to communicate with the financial markets. They are happy to take the bondholders' money to finance their excessive deficits, and then act outraged when those bondholders retreat and push up interest rates."[6]

To Tilford's and Münchau's arguments, Marco Annunziata, chief economist of the Italian bank UniCredit, added,

> eurozone policymakers should stop to consider that the markets are not just a collection of greedy speculators. Especially in the case of sovereign bonds, the markets are in large part made up of pension funds and insurance companies trying to protect the value of their investments, so they can honor their liabilities to retirees and other citizens. When these investors develop concerns about the risk of sovereign bonds, they should be listened to, not treated as the enemy.[7]

The "the markets do not understand" argument brought the verbal gymnastics of European officials to a new level of sophistication. Remarkably—but also understandably, from a political perspective—few European officials openly admitted to what by 2010 had become obvious. Van Rompuy was a notable exception. "The foundation of the euro," he declared at the end of 2010, "has been kept too small... With one currency, we need to integrate more politically, but in reality we did just the opposite."[8] The problems with the euro and the European monetary union in general are structural and systemic in nature. *The End of the Euro* intends to place this statement into the correct historical perspective.

Europe's Economic and Monetary Union (EMU) began as a political project. Twice during the twentieth century, the European

continent was devastated by war. Hoping to prevent a similar ca-
lamity, post–World War II leaders and intellectuals collaborated to
create European unification. The task was complicated, of course,
by the Cold War going on between the United States and the Soviet Union and the Iron Curtain that divided the continent. Over
the decades, it became more and more obvious that nationalistic
reflexes stood in the way of direct political union among the major
European countries. However, a workable economic and monetary
consensus among the noncommunist Western European countries
seemed possible. The European Economic Community, which was
created in 1957, was focused on establishing an economic union.

In the slipstream of the 1989 reunification of Germany, French
President François Mitterrand convinced German Chancellor
Helmut Kohl into acceptance of a monetary union. Mitterrand's
political acumen led to the realization of a dream the French elite
had cherished for decades: breaking German monetary hegemony
and curbing the dominance of the Bundesbank, the German central bank, over Europe's monetary and economic destiny. As former British prime minister John Major remarked, "The difference
between the French position and ours in 1992 was that the whole
French establishment wanted the single currency as a means of ty-
ing down Leviathan, of binding the Bundesbank."[9]

Despite the fact that they were unable to parallel Germany's
economic progress, the French were still thoroughly convinced
that they should play a leading role in European and world affairs. They saw Europe as the only available venue for the realization of their strategic objectives. Since monetary and exchange rate
policies were the only field in which a broad European consensus
seemed feasible, French politicians seized the opportunity.

The Maastricht Treaty of December 1991 was the first step in
a process that eventually led to the 1999 formation of a monetary
union among eleven Western European countries. The union's

single currency became the euro and the European Central Bank (ECB) became its sole policymaking central bank.

Economists recognized from the start that imbalances among the union's member countries existed—imbalances that could threaten the entire project. To prevent this, they argued, a set of conditions needed to be fulfilled. Based on the relatively well-established economic theory of the optimum currency area (OCA), these conditions included the existence of a political and fiscal union and sufficient mobility and flexibility in the labor markets.

The political elite paid elaborate lip service to these warnings, while at the same time insisting that these conditions were unnecessary. Showing persistence and unity, they claimed, would automatically turn the EMU into a strong monetary union—and furthermore, the political cooperation required to operate the EMU project efficiently would lead to political unification.

With this reasoning as their basis, the political elite supervising the project turned a great idea into a huge gamble. The idea that Europe's leading politicians could solve any crisis that popped up was arguably the cornerstone of their plan. Former Belgian prime minister and European heavyweight Jean-Luc Dehaene stated, "The idea of a unified Europe grows and becomes reality through crises. We need crises to make progress." Dehaene and like-minded European politicians never seriously considered the possibility of an insoluble, catastrophic crisis potentially crashing the euro system and even the whole idea of European integration.

From 1999 to 2008, the politicians' claims seemed valid. While there was little substantial progress toward real political union, the euro itself and the euro countries in general prospered. Despite tumultuous events worldwide, such as the bursting of the dot-com bubble, the 9/11 terrorist attacks, and the wars in Afghanistan and Iraq, no major crisis befell the EMU during the early years of its existence.

The financial crisis of 2007–2009 dramatically changed that situation. In January 2009, Barry Eichengreen, professor of economics and political science at the University of California, Berkeley, accurately wrote that "what started as the Subprime Crisis in 2007 and morphed in the Global Credit Crisis in 2008 has become the Euro Crisis in 2009."[10]

Blindness to risk had characterized the years preceding the financial meltdown, but during the period that immediately followed, risk aversion spread like a virus through the financial and banking systems. The financial and capital markets soon started to worry about sovereign risks (i.e., the risk of countries becoming insolvent). Although budget deficits in countries like the United States and the United Kingdom were much larger than in the euro area, markets started to focus on EMU countries.

This observation, of course, means that budgetary excesses are not the only factor causing concern about the euro's future, a theme we'll explore in Chapter 2. Markets increasingly recognized that the problem was the monetary union itself. Eichengreen's "euro crisis" revolves around the sustainability of the EMU and the single currency. The problems threatening the EMU and the euro have little to do with speculative attacks or the behavior of the financial markets, or even with the financial crisis. Despite the finger-pointing among Europe's political elite, the EMU construct was an accident waiting to happen. A major crisis was unavoidable.

The treaties, pacts, and political agreements that created the EMU and guided its development produced untenable internal and external imbalances within the monetary union. Politicians' failure to act on this reality and ensure that the union functioned smoothly makes them the primary culprits.

Chapter 1 of *The End of the Euro* deals with the euro's birth, but begins way before that. We start in the nineteenth century, but the main focus is the post–World War II era. Monetary union was then seen as a means to an end. The mainstream argument was that monetary union would give gradual rise to a political union and the continent could finally end its long history of war and destruction. You will need a clear understanding of this historical background to understand the anomalies built into the EMU project from the beginning.

The EMU is not an optimum currency area—in fact, it's far from it, as discussed in Chapter 2. It lacks, among other things, a strong political union with transparent and automatic fiscal transfers and flexible labor markets. The pages of Chapter 2 confront these anomalies with insights gained from the economic analysis of optimum currency areas.

Chapter 3 describes the euro crisis as it has waged on since late 2009, including detail on how it came about as a result of structural flaws. While the euro's tailspin was an accident waiting to happen, the surprise is that it took a decade to take place. Once the crisis gained momentum, European authorities hesitated. They lost themselves in short-term band-aid packages and never really gained control of the situation, despite endless meetings and summits. As the *Financial Times* put it during the spring of 2011, "Throughout the financial crisis, Europe's elected leaders have rarely missed an opportunity to disappoint."[11]

The interventions on the part of the European authorities were invariably of the "too little, too late" variety, and the leaders seemed to actively avoid the major issues, such as the structural weakness of the European banking sector and the contradictions in programs imposed on member countries. The euro crisis will continue until one of two things happens:

1. The EMU becomes a full-fledged political union (hence, also a fiscal and transfer union) with much more flexible and mobile labor markets.
2. The whole thing unravels.

The acute crises in smaller countries, like Greece, Portugal, and Ireland, are serious but unlikely to fundamentally endanger the euro. This would change, however, if larger and more populous countries, such as Spain or Italy, experienced similar crises. Chapter 4 argues that the more likely outcome is that mighty Germany will put the euro out of its misery. While German officials remain outspokenly pro-euro, the German people are becoming critical, and even outright hostile, to the union and its currency. Germany's deeply entrenched culture of monetary stability increasingly conflicts with the way the eurozone and its central bank are being run. Unless the management of the euro is brought more in line with Germany's culture of stability, Germans will pull the plug and bring about the end of the euro as we know it today.

Chapter 1

The long march

From conception, through gestation, birth, and into its early infancy, the euro has consistently proved the sceptics wrong. Some thought that chauvinistic voters would reject the single currency in referenda. Others doubted that all the applicants would fulfill the Maastricht deficit criterion. Still others predicted that disputes over the European Central Bank's presidency might abort the enterprise. Yet, Economic and Monetary Union has thus far proceeded according to plan.

BRITISH HISTORIAN NIALL FERGUSON WROTE THESE words in 2001.[12] Skepticism about the chances for success of the EMU and the euro was widespread, and not only among Anglo-Saxon economists and commentators.

"It can't happen. It's a bad idea. It won't last." So the Anglo-Saxon attitude was summarized in late 2009.[13] This skepticism was understandable, given past failed attempts to create a durable monetary union in Europe. A brief look at some pre-1945 initiatives, specifically the German monetary unification (which succeeded) and the Latin and Scandinivian Monetary Unions (both of which failed) illustrates the lessons to be drawn from these experiences.

Bismarck's Power Play

In 1996, Dutch monetary historian Wim Vanthoor wrote,

> Two thousand years of European history bear witness to
> continual attempts to convert Europe, united as it had
> been in terms of culture and civilization since the very
> beginnings of our era, into a political and economic
> union. Philosophers and poets alike sang the praises of
> a united Europe.[14]

Attempts at monetary unification on the European continent
date as far back as ancient Greece, and the history books are rich
with examples. However, a strict definition of a monetary union
confines those comparisons. It must involve an agreement between
two or more countries that meets at least three conditions:

1. There must either be a single currency or several currencies linked to each other at immutably fixed exchange
   rates.
2. Only one exchange rate may exist between the union
   currency and each other currency in existence.
3. All countries in the union must follow one monetary
   policy.[15]

By this definition, the oldest successful monetary union was
probably the one between Massachusetts, New Hampshire, Con-
necticut, and Rhode Island between roughly 1650 and 1750 (although these colonies could not really be considered individual
and independent states).[16] Obviously, the United States is an excellent example of a successful attempt.[17]

In Europe, the first major successful attempt at monetary union
was made in what is now Germany.[18] (Similar processes took place
in Italy and Switzerland, but the German example is the most rel-
evant.[19]) Despite continuous attempts at political unification, by

the early nineteenth century the German Federation still consisted of thirty-nine independent states, each with its own currency. With the exception of Prussia, these countries were small and far behind in terms of economic development. Political and economic leaders realized that this fragmentation hindered trade and movement. In 1838, a few years after the creation of a customs union (*Zollverein*) that removed most of the existing trade barriers, the members of the German Federation agreed on two monetary standards: the Thaler, used mainly by the northern states, and the Gulden, used mainly by the southern states.

A decade later, the central bank of Prussia, the Preussische Bank, took over the monetary policy for most of the states. Prussia's monetary leadership, along with its sheer size and power, allowed it to enforce compliance on the smaller states and hold the monetary union together.[20] Prussia's victory over France in 1871 gave Otto von Bismarck the authority to push through political unification, creating the German Reich.[21] Four years later, the Preussische Bank was transformed into the Reichsbank. The German monetary system shifted to a gold standard, to which the whole German territory adhered by the start of 1876. After World War II, the Reichsbank was reshaped into the Bundesbank (sometimes affectionately called the "Buba"), the institution that became the dominant central bank in Western Europe by the 1960s.

German monetary unification largely preceded political unification. The EMU sought to follow the same process. But more than a decade after its inception, political union is not yet on the horizon. No single state in twenty-first-century Europe has had the power or ruthlessness of Bismarck's Prussia, under whose leadership nineteenth-century Germany was already a de facto political union.

Latin Bazaar

The German experience, however, does not precisely fit our definition of a monetary union, which specifies an agreement between two or more independent countries. The German states had already formed a customs union and shared a common culture and history. Nationalistic sentiments, combined with fortunate historical circumstances and Bismarck's determined initiative, paved the way to a politically unified Germany.

In contrast, the Latin Monetary Union (LMU), formed in August 1866, was an attempt to assemble a monetary union from a group of independent states. Led by France, the LMU initially included Belgium, Italy, and Switzerland, with Greece joining three years later. Upon the formation of the LMU, Walter Bagehot, the legendary founding editor of the renowned British weekly *The Economist*, claimed that "before long, all Europe, save England, will have one money."[22]

While this was certainly a visionary idea, Bagehot had based it on an unfortunate example. The LMU grew out of a monetary partnership that had already existed for several decades and used the monetary model of France. Napoleon Bonaparte's Coinage Act of 1803 placed France on a bimetallic standard, minting both gold and silver coins. With France as their main trading and financial partner, Belgium, Italy, and Switzerland followed the same practice, and their central banks guaranteed to exchange gold and silver for coins.[23]

Two developments placed strain on the bimetallic standard. First, the price of gold fell substantially in the early 1850s. Pressure on the relative prices of gold and silver naturally followed, and the divergent prices led to destabilizing flows of gold and silver. Second, the countries involved began minting coins of varying metal content, mostly because of the price divergences. The LMU's main purpose was to establish uniform coinage standards, thus paving the way for a larger economic area, where gold and silver coins could circulate freely.

There was much more to the LMU than simply a desire for better monetary arrangements. In 1867, the French government organized an international conference designed to persuade the prominent countries in the world economy to accept the bimetallic standard—and nothing came of it. According to Vanthoor, France considered the LMU "the nucleus of an international monetary system centering on the double standard.... The French government fervently advocated the double standard, hoping, among other things, to expand its economic and political power beyond its borders."[24] France's defeat in the Franco–Prussian War was a major blow to the country's international ambitions.

The fact that the participating countries never established a common monetary standard was the downfall of the LMU. Each country kept its own central bank. Under these conditions, the obligation for each central bank to accept the other countries' coins at par and without limit regularly destabilized capital flows. Another issue was "the insufficient convergence of the policies conducted by the member states. As a result, the country abiding by the rules most stringently was inevitably flooded by speculative capital flowing from member states whose currencies felt the pressure of their expansionary spending policies."[25] During World War I, the spending policies of the LMU countries diverged even more, and some members opted for large-scale money creation to finance that spending. Currency depreciation inevitably followed. Although the LMU ended formally in 1927, it had essentially failed during World War I.

Scandinavian Failure

The Scandinavian Monetary Union (SMU) followed a similar trajectory.[26] Sweden and Denmark formally entered into a monetary union in 1872, and Norway joined in 1875. The ultimate intention of these already closely related countries was to form a political and economic union, and the nations believed stable monetary relations were a prerequisite.[27] The three countries already adhered to the silver standard and accepted each other's coins and banknotes, which simplified the process. It was feared that the newly formed German state's choice of a gold standard would lead to a substantial decline in the value of silver.

The SMU fixed the exchange rates of the Swedish crown, the Danish crown, and the Norwegian crown in terms a specific amount of gold. Leaving the silver standard behind allowed the SMU to avoid the bimetallism problems that had handicapped the LMU.

The Scandinavian nations exhibited considerable discipline in adhering to the rules upon which they had agreed. Monetary cooperation between the three central banks allowed the SMU to function smoothly during the first three decades of its existence. By the end of the nineteenth century, banks in each country accepted the other members' banknotes at par, and the monetary union was considered complete.

However, problems began to surface in 1905, when Norway demanded full political independence from Sweden, and Denmark's more restrictive policies attracted capital flows from the two other SMU members. Ultimately, World War I proved lethal to the SMU. Pressed by the circumstances of the war, each country gradually created its own monetary and budgetary policies.

By the end of 1915, Sweden had terminated the parity agreement with Denmark and Norway. Large amounts of gold flowing into the Scandinavian countries accelerated the disintegration of the monetary union. In 1924, the member countries agreed that the coins of each country were no longer legal tender in the partner countries—essentially ending the SMU (the official end came six years later, when the three countries left the gold standard).

The failure of the SMU holds important lessons for a modern-day monetary union in Europe. The Scandinavian countries were already integrated politically, economically, culturally, and monetarily when they started a full monetary union. Despite the fact that they started off with a fairly united front, their independent political authorities created monetary and budgetary policies that proved incompatible with the union. Much like the LMU, the SMU was undone by a lack of binding, enforceable agreements and mechanisms to coordinate monetary policy and economic policy in general. The twin failures of the SMU and the LMU prove that a durable monetary union is hard to achieve without parallel movement toward political union.

Between politically sovereign states, Vanthoor remarked, "monetary union is only sustainable and irreversible if it is embedded in a political union, in which competences beyond the monetary sphere are also transferred to a supranational body.... The will to adjust was limited or non-existent, due to the fact that there was no political structure enforcing such a will."[28]

In the early 1990s, Marcus Lusser, who at that time was governor of the Swiss National Bank, made a similar argument:

> Probably, those historical monetary unions could have survived if there had been a system of financial compensation (*Finanzausgleich*) among the participating countries. However, such a compensation system requires a degree of political solidarity that can only be reached within a political union.[29]

In a similar vein, economic historian Michael Bordo refers to

> a key difference between the success rates of national monetary unions like the United States, Canada, Germany, and Italy compared with international monetary unions like the Scandinavian Monetary Union and the

Latin Monetary Union. The key reasons for this outcome were the force of political will and greater economic integration. In case of national monetary unions, monetary integration was an integral part of the process of creating a nation state.[30]

Monetary integration attempts in Europe were halted between 1914 and 1945 by two devastating wars, both of which were fought largely on European soil, and an interbellum period of uncertainty and turmoil. The Roaring Twenties led almost overnight to the agony and misery of the Great Depression, and during the same period, Hitler's rise to power in Germany provoked a human catastrophe without precedent. When World War II ended, European leaders were determined to prevent these events from ever happening again.

The Road to Rome

To prevent future catastrophes on European soil, the continent's leaders needed to end the struggle for dominance between Germany and France. British Prime Minister Winston Churchill declared in September 1946 that "a kind of United States of Europe" was absolutely necessary to prevent new wars.[31]

The U.S. also pushed for greater unity among the Western European countries, in part to create a significant counterweight to the communist bloc Stalin had formed in the eastern part of the continent. Germany, for example, had been divided into two countries. West Germany fell under the American influence, and communist East Germany became a satellite state of the Soviet Union. Americans' Cold War logic had quickly led to a situation where "initial Allied hesitation on whether to rebuild or run down West Germany's industrial fabric gave way to pragmatic insistence on renewal."[32]

The U.S.-launched European Recovery Programme, better known as the Marshall Plan,[33] explicitly required European countries to consult with each other over the use of American funds.[34]

This led to the creation of the Organization for European Economic Co-operation (OEEC).[35] In 1950, the OEEC gave rise to the European Payments Union, an agreement that facilitated intra-European trade and payments and aimed to restore the convertibility of European currencies.

Jean Monnet, then the head of the French Planning Agency (*Commissariat du Plan*), was convinced that international control of France and Germany's heavy industries was needed to avoid future armed conflicts between the two countries. In 1951, Monnet's vision became official French policy in the form of the European Coal and Steel Community (ECSC). The ECSC created a common market for coal and steel among West Germany, France, Italy, the Netherlands, Belgium, and Luxembourg. France's minister of foreign affairs, Robert Schuman, made no secret of his belief that the ECSC should be considered a first step toward a more complete European federation. However, attempts to step up the pace of integration were unsuccessful; for example, initiatives to create a European Defence Council ended in failure in 1954.

The Suez crisis of 1956 sharply underlined the need for greater European unity if the old continent intended to remain a major player on the world scene. During the crisis, the European countries had no option but to obey American instructions. Shortly after the Americans forced the British and the French to abandon their attack on the Suez Canal, West Germany's first chancellor, Konrad Adenauer, remarked to Christian Pineau, France's foreign minister, "France and England will never be powers comparable to the United States and the Soviet Union. Nor Germany, either. There remains to them only one way of playing a decisive role in the world: that is to unite to make Europe."[36]

By the mid-1950s, Western European leaders had realized that the economic sphere was the best path to political union, and some had very explicit ideas. In 1950, Jacques Rueff, a French economist and longtime advisor to French President General Charles de Gaulle, declared, *"L'Europe se fera par la monnaie, ou ne se fera pas."* ("Europe shall be made through the currency or it shall not be made at all.")[37] Rueff's vision was clearly present in the Spaak Report, which arose from the June 1955 Messina conference.[38] To advance the unification of Europe, the Spaak Report pleaded for closer economic cooperation and the creation of a common market.

On March 25, 1957, the leading politicians of the six ECSC countries met in Rome to create the European Atomic Energy Community (Euratom) and the European Economic Community (EEC); the European Commission was subsequently set up to run the daily affairs of the EEC. The aim of the EEC was no less than the full integration of the whole economy of its six founding member countries (West Germany, France, Italy, the Netherlands, Belgium and Luxembourg). The plan was to eliminate trade tariffs and free up the movement of goods, services, people, and capital. Although the focus was on economic integration, there was little doubt that, in the words of professor of European studies David Coombes, "the Treaty (of Rome)…clearly…intended to lead eventually to a political union."[39]

The Monetary Committee was established in March 1958, following the Treaty of Rome. This committee was tasked with coordinating the monetary policies of the EEC member states, and its members included the nations' respective ministers of finance and the central banks. In 1964, the Committee of Central Bank Governors was set up with a similar goal.

In 1962, the Common Agricultural Policy (CAP) of the EEC began. The CAP was characterized by a complex system of farm support prices that especially benefitted French farmers. By the mid-1960s, fluctuating currency values had endangered the CAP system, so it was no surprise that Robert Marjolin, the French member of the European Commission, argued strongly for the elimination of currency fluctuations within the EEC. He declared in 1965 that monetary union was "an inevitable obligation."[40]

Werner's Plan

In 1969, the European Commission issued a memorandum urging an intensification of the economic and monetary coordination in Europe. This memorandum came to be known as the Barre Plan, after Commission vice president and, later, prime minister of France Raymond Barre. It was no coincidence that a French technocrat was the driving force behind this memorandum, as the French were becoming increasingly aware that the only way to gain influence over the economic powerhouse on France's Eastern border was through a European initiative.

The Germans, supported by the Dutch, reacted hesitantly to the Barre Plan—the main reason being that the Plan called for the convergence of economic policies of the member states. The German authorities were not prepared to compromise on their economic policies. In those years, Germany indeed outperformed the other EEC countries, including France. Its conservative fiscal and monetary policies led to high levels of employment, low and stable inflation, and higher personal income levels. The more left-leaning governments in most other European countries generally disliked the conservative German policies.

Despite their cool reception of the Barre Plan, the Germans showed interest in monetary union because of what they perceived as the "dollar problem." International monetary tensions were escalating rapidly by the end of the 1960s, and the United States' inflationary policies undermined the stability of the dollar, the currency that anchored the postwar international monetary order.[41] By the late 1950s, Otmar Emminger, the member of the Bundesbank Directorate responsible for international monetary affairs (he was later made president of the Bundesbank), was already pleading for a revaluation of the Deutsche mark (D-mark) to safeguard Germany from U.S. inflationary policies.[42] After a heated debate between the Bundesbank and the government of Adenauer, who was concerned about the effects of restrictive monetary policies on growth and employment, the D-mark and the Dutch guilder were revaluated by 5 percent in 1961.

Agreement was reached at the December 1969 EEC Summit in The Hague to have a commission chaired by Pierre Werner, the prime minister of Luxembourg, draw up a plan for the gradual realization of the EMU.

The Werner Plan was published in October 1970. David Marsh, author of several books on monetary integration in Europe, described it as "festooned with opaque language and studded with half-hearted compromises."[43] It was indeed a mish-mash of different ideas on the creation of a monetary union. These differences have yet to be reconciled. The basic contrast is between the northern vision, embodied by Germany and the Netherlands, and the southern vision, as articulated by France and Italy.

The Werner Plan laid out a ten-year, three-stage timeline for the creation of the EMU.[44] The first stage would restrict exchange rate fluctuations and intensify the coordination of monetary and fiscal policies among the member states. During the second stage, exchange rate fluctuations and divergences in price movements would be further reduced. The third and final stage of EMU would permanently fix exchange rates and establish a community-wide system of central banks. The discussions surrounding the Werner Plan drew a clear line between the Germans, who were supported consistently by the Dutch, and the French, who could usually count on support from Italy and Belgium.

Part of the problem for the Germans was that the D-mark had become a symbol of the prosperity and dignity the country had regained since World War II. Chancellor Helmut Kohl said in 1985,

"The D-mark is our flag. It is the fundament of our post-war reconstruction. It is the essential part of our national pride; we don't have much else."[45]

Even French politicians understood their reluctance to give it up. "The mark is the manifestation of German power. This is a very deep issue that transcends the reflexes of bankers, and goes even beyond politics," Mitterrand admitted in 1987.[46]

The Germans' fundamental argument was that a successful monetary union required the simultaneous creation of a political union. The Germans still stood squarely behind the opinion voiced by Bundesbank president Karl Blessing in the early 1960s that monetary union required "a common trade policy, a common finance and budget policy, a common economic policy, a common social and wage policy—a common policy all around"[47]—in short, the kind of policy coordination that is hard to imagine without a full-scale political union.

Germany's insistence on the need for a political union was a constant in the decade-long discussion about monetary union. Furthermore, German politicians, central bankers, and economists often gave the impression that they insisted on this issue because political union was unreachable—hence, the argument was a clever way to block the road to monetary union.

The Germans also cherished the concept of a central bank independent of political influence. To prevent a repetition of the monetary and economic chaos of the 1920s and 1930s, the Bundesbank Law of 1957 explicitly stipulated independence of the central bank from the political government. The Germans insisted on the same kind of independence for a European central bank.

The French, on the other hand, rejected the prospect of transferring substantial national policy prerogatives to the European level. They believed that a central bank would ultimately fall under the supervision of political authorities. The French focused on the first

stage of the Werner Plan, relentlessly stressing that deficit and surplus countries had an equal responsibility to come to convergence.
Acceptance of this argument would have meant that Germany (the
traditional surplus country, together with the Netherlands) could
not impose its policies on France and Italy (the traditional deficit
countries). Today, more than forty years after the Werner Plan, these
differences between Germany and France remain intact.

Of Snakes and Tunnels

In March 1971, the Council of Ministers, the most important
decision-making body within the EEC, adopted a watered-down
version of the Werner Plan. The Council consisted of the heads of
state and government leaders of the six member countries. From
the start, international money upheavals complicated the goal of
narrowing the fluctuation margins of the exchange rates of the six
EEC currencies.[48]

These upheavals led to the May 1971 decision to let the German mark float on the currency markets and culminated in the
Nixon administration's August 1971 suspension of the dollar's gold
convertibility. This decision immediately set the dollar on a steep
devaluation path. In March 1972, the mutual fluctuation margin
around the parities of the EEC currencies was narrowed to 2.25
percent—an agreement labeled the "snake in the tunnel."[49] Denmark, Ireland, and the United Kingdom joined the EEC in this
arrangement on January 1, 1973, bringing the total membership to
nine countries.[50]

The European snake was freed from its tunnel in early 1973,
when the United States let the dollar float vis-à-vis the most important currencies. Several currencies opted out of the snake, and
some returned. Overall, as Vanthoor concluded, "the objective of the
Werner Report came to nothing."[51] Insufficient coordination of economic and monetary policies was the major reason for this failure.

The criticism from a working group set up by the European Commission and chaired by Robert Marjolin was even harsher: "Europe is no nearer to EMU than in 1969. In fact, if there has been any movement, it has been backward: national economic and monetary policies have never in 25 years been more discordant, more divergent than they are today."[52]

The failure of the Werner Plan was just one manifestation of the underlying problem: Almost no one was thinking (or acting) in Europe's best interest. Most leaders sought to use the project to their countries' advantage. In particular, France and Germany remained focused on their own interests. Today, more than a decade into the twenty-first century, these countries still find their nationalistic reflexes difficult to overcome.

The snake arrangement hobbled along as currencies left and returned (the French franc, for example, did so several times) and currencies revalued and devalued. Reactions to the first major oil crisis in 1973–74 contributed to the chaos. While the Germans followed more traditional policies, trying to rein in inflation and excessive budget deficits, most of the other EEC countries fought the recession by increasing government spending and deficits. Instead of a monetary union, Europe ended up with a de facto D-mark bloc. David Marsh remarked, "The Bundesbank's floating currency policy was victorious. The European Community (EC) was becalmed and rudderless."[53]

EMS-ing

During the spring of 1978, German Chancellor Helmut Schmidt and French President Valéry Giscard d'Estaing, both former ministers of finance, agreed that something needed to be done to restore monetary calm. The French were, as always, on the lookout for ways to reduce German dominance. Giscard was quite explicit about this issue: "I want France to ensure that there are in Europe at least two countries of comparable influence, Germany and France.... We need an organised Europe to escape German domination."[54] The Germans, on the other hand, were increasingly concerned about the capital flight of the dollar in the D-mark. The upward pressure on the D-mark created major difficulties for Germany's export-driven model of economic growth and made an independent monetary policy based on the national needs of Germany much more difficult to execute.[55] Moreover, Schmidt feared that outright German domination in the monetary and economic fields might produce political disadvantages.[56]

Schmidt and d'Estaing provided the political drive, but the work was mainly done by three technocrats: Horst Schulmann, Schmidt's closest advisor; Bernard Clappier, governor of the Banque de France and Giscard's *confidante*; and the Belgian Jacques van Ypersele de Strihou, who was chairman of the Monetary Committee from 1978 to 1979 and who worked hard to bring France and Germany to a compromise.[57] Roy Jenkins, the Brit who presided over the European Commission from 1977 to 1981, described Schulmann and Clappier, who were thriving on the unconditional support they enjoyed from Schmidt and Giscard, as deciding everything "above the heads" of all the others.[58]

The European Monetary System (EMS) was launched on January 1, 1979. At its core was the Exchange Rate Mechanism (ERM), which fixed bilateral parities between all the currencies involved. The fluctuation margins around these parities were fixed at +/– 2.25 percent. (The Italian lira was given a fluctuation margin of +/– 6 percent due to Italy's higher inflation rate.) Great Britain joined the EMS but kept the pound out of the ERM. The EMS also created the European Currency Unit (ECU), a *numéraire*, or artificial currency unit, based on the value of the EMS currencies. Each currency contributed to the value of the ECU according to the economic weight of the country.

In an attempt to neutralize Germany's dominance, the French tried to maneuver the ECU into a central role within the EMS, but the Germans skillfully countered. Not without *Schadenfreude*, Karl Otto Pöhl, who in those days was vice president of the Bundesbank, later recalled that "the Bundesbank turned the original concept [for the EMS] on its head by making the strongest currency the yardstick of the system."[59] The German dominance was explicitly confirmed by the late Italian economist, minister of finance, and central banker Tommaso Padoa-Schioppa: "Between the early 1970s and late 1990s, the D-mark replaced the dollar as the anchor of European currencies."[60]

In the negotiations that led to the creation of the EMS, there was much discussion about who would support the weaker currencies. Predictably, the French felt that the surplus countries should support the weaker currencies as well, and the Germans disagreed. The so-called Belgian compromise, devised by Jacques van Ypersele, used a divergence indicator to determine responsibility. This mechanism never really worked. The dominance of the D-mark and the Bundesbank meant that if one or more currencies came under pressure, the Bundesbank could simply decide not to intervene.

The severe recession that followed the second major oil crisis of 1979–80, as well as the French socialist experiment, led to several years of continuous upheaval within the EMS. The newly elected president of France, Mitterrand, wanted to show that there was an alternative to the free market policies pursued by Ronald Reagan in the United States and Margaret Thatcher in Great Britain. He launched a drastic new economic policy based on nationalizations and massive fiscal stimulus (essentially through higher government expenditures). These policies soon resulted in higher inflation, increasing unemployment, rising social tensions and strikes, deficits on the trade balance, escalating budget deficits, and continuous pressure on the French franc inside the EMS. Several devaluations of the French franc were necessary—sometimes alone, and sometimes with the Italian lira and the Belgian franc.

As a result, French frustration with the Germans' hard currency policies reached new levels. France even contemplated leaving the ERM in early 1983, but the nation's minister of finance, Jacques Delors, finally convinced Mitterrand and the rest of the French government that the nation's economic and monetary policies needed a fundamental redesign. Delors started to rebuild these policies more along the orthodox German lines, and early in 1987, the French franc devalued one last time. The objective of a *franc fort* (a strong franc) closely linked to the D-mark in the foreign exchange markets became a cornerstone of French government policy.[61] The socialists' defeat by the Gaullists and conservatives in the parliamentary elections of March 1986 played a key role in this policy evolution. Mitterrand was obliged to compromise on his socialist principles.

After the last French devaluation, a remarkable period of calm descended on the EMS. Differences in inflation rates between the member countries had decreased considerably, making adjustments in currency parities less necessary, and the Basel-Nyborg consensus, which would follow, served as another stabilizing factor.

In September 1987, the central bankers of the EMS countries met in the Swiss city of Basel, home to the Bank for International Settlements (the bank of central bankers), and agreed that the exchange rates within the EMS needed to be kept fixed. Monetary policy was to be adjusted in terms of this objective—to put it in the jargon of economists, it was accepted that external equilibrium (a fixed exchange rate) was more important than internal equilibrium (growth and employment). The agreement also included additional financial means to intervene when exchange rates came under pressure in the markets. A few days later, this principle was underwritten by a meeting of ministers of finance in the Danish town of Nyborg. Markets were impressed with this new consensus, and over time they became even more impressed by the political resolve in the European monetary sphere.

Enter Jacques

Meanwhile, Europe was undergoing a rapid transformation. In 1985, Delors was appointed as president of the European Commission. Delors immediately set out to revise the original EEC Treaty, but Germany, the Netherlands, and Great Britain blocked his subtle attempts to include the EMS.

Nevertheless, he succeeded in reaching an overall agreement on the Single European Act, which took effect on July 1, 1987. This act stipulated complete freedom of intracommunity movements of services and capital transactions by 1992. Optimistic as a result of this success, Delors started pushing for monetary unification.[62] Once again, the all-consuming French desire to break Germany's monetary dominance was the impetus of the attempt.

The European Council decided at its June 1988 summit to set up a Committee of Experts (with Delors at its helm) to manage the economic and monetary union. The committee was asked to submit concrete proposals by the following year's summit. The ultimate intention of the French was to divide the decision-making power of the Bundesbank among all European central bankers.

Of course, the Bundesbank strongly objected, but for political reasons, Germany's minister of foreign affairs, Hans-Dietrich Genscher, did not really oppose France's intentions. Genscher sensed that fundamental changes were coming in Central and Eastern Europe.[63] If Germany was to reclaim its historic role in that region without reviving too explicitly the demons of its war-filled past, Genscher felt that the country needed to build up goodwill with its Western European partners, especially the French and the British. Genscher's feeling about the future of the communist East was soon proven correct.

In April 1989, Delors presented his report on the realization of the EMU.[64] Central to the Delors Report was the argument that monetary union should be viewed as a "natural, indeed unavoidable, consequence of the Single Act."[65] This premise was largely based on the impossible trinity, or trilemma, principle.[66] Monetary theory and historical experience show that of three basic goals—fixed exchange rates, capital mobility, and autonomous monetary policies—only two can be pursued simultaneously. Following an independent monetary policy obliges a country to give up on either capital mobility or a fixed exchange rate. If exchange rates are flexible, a combination of an autonomous monetary policy and full capital mobility is possible.[67] If you want a fixed exchange rate and capital mobility (both of which are basic characteristics of a monetary union), you must give up on an autonomous monetary policy.

Like the Werner Plan, the Delors Report planned the creation of the EMU in three stages over a period of ten years. The main difference was that the Werner Plan went further in transferring national budgetary competences to the EEC level. The final aim of the Delors Plan was fixed exchange rates and a single monetary policy for the EMU, to be conducted by the European System of Central Banks (ESCB). Replacement of the national currencies by a single European currency was included as an option.

All in all, David Marsh concluded, "the Delors document resembled a giant jigsaw puzzle where many important parts were missing. There were few clues where they might be and only a vague timetable for finding them."[68] Pöhl, who was also a member of the Delors Committee, described the report as "a confused piece of work."[69] The need to compromise politically resulted in economic inconsistencies and even outright fallacies in the architecture of the monetary union—a recurring theme in the EMU's birth process.

Mitterrand Playing Hardball

Among the twelve member states of the EC, the British opposed the Delors Plan most fervently. German opposition to the Delors Plan became much less pronounced as a consequence of Mitterrand's clever geopolitical strategy. Genscher's subtle signals and gestures for a political tit-for-tat had not been lost on the astute French president, who nearly a decade before the fall of the Berlin Wall had realized that a reunified Germany was inevitable.

World War II veteran Mitterrand didn't like the idea of a reunified Germany, but he knew he couldn't stop it, either. So the French president chose to make the most of the situation. Although Mitterrand was hardly interested in monetary and economic affairs, he saw the possibility of a major strategic tradeoff and pursued the strategy with his usual ruthlessness.[70]

The well-respected German economist Hans-Werner Sinn has the following to say on this episode: "When Chancellor Kohl and President Mitterrand announced in early 1990 that there would be a government conference in Maastricht, Mitterrand also promised his support for the unification of Germany. This was a surprising step, given that in late 1989 Mitterrand had tried his utmost to prevent that unification. He had tried hard to stabilize the east German regime and to persuade Gorbachev to veto the unification, but without success. *It is an open secret that Germany had to buy the consent of France by sacrificing the deutschmark* (italics mine)." [71] Michel Rocard, French prime minister from 1988 to 1991, put it somewhat less bluntly: "There was a balance between unification of Germany and the establishment of European monetary union…. Mitterrand had to accept reunification more quickly than he thought likely, in the same way that Kohl had to accept monetary union more quickly than he intended."[72]

Comments made by Thatcher, Mitterrand, and Kohl in their respective memoirs give considerable support to Sinn's argument and the balancing act to which Rocard referred. According to Thatcher, "awareness of the past and uncertainty about the future led President Mitterrand and me, with not very effective assistance from President Gorbachev, to try to slow down the rush to German unification. In the end, we failed."[73] David Marsh describes a March 1990 meeting between Thatcher and a delegation of historians, during which Thatcher sympathized with the view that a reunified Germany would be a belligerent Germany. According to Charles Powell, Thatcher's private secretary, the consensus was that Germans were prone to "angst, aggressiveness, assertiveness, bullying, egotism, inferiority complex, sentimentality."[74] In his memoirs, Helmut Kohl claimed that "what I could only guess at then is now proven, with the opening of the archives. Margaret Thatcher wanted to hinder German unity with all possible means."[75] In the same breath, Kohl accused Mitterrand of double crossing him several times.

Under the leadership of Kohl and Mitterrand, who had first seriously discussed the prospect of monetary union in the autumn of 1985, things started to move rapidly in late 1989. On November 28, 1989, Kohl presented to the German parliament his ten-point plan for German unification, to the surprise of other European leaders. On November 30, German Foreign Minister Hans-Dietrich Genscher faced a furious Mitterrand at the Elysée Palace in Paris. Mitterrand wanted immediate German agreement on monetary union in Europe. If this did not happen, he threatened, he would force Germany into isolation vis-à-vis a united front of France, Britain, and the Soviet Union.[76] "Under this extreme threat," concluded David Marsh, "Kohl backed down."[77]

Several summits of the European Council, two intergovernmental conferences looking into possible amendments to the EEC treaty, and extensive discussion on different levels regarding the timing and precise content of the stages of EMU and the nature of the ESCB finally led to a European Council meeting in the Dutch city of Maastricht in early December 1991. The Maastricht treaty, formally signed on February 7, 1992, contained a new framework for a political, economic, and monetary union in the EC. The approach was based on gradualism and convergence.

The Maastricht Mantra

The gradualist aspect of the Maastricht Treaty was reflected in the three-stage approach to launching the EMU:

1. Stage One, set to begin on July 1, 1990, was characterized by complete freedom of capital movement in Europe, increased cooperation and coordination with respect to convergence, and the preparatory work for Stage Three.
2. Stage Two, set to start on January 1, 1994, included the establishment of the European Monetary Institute (EMI), the forerunner of the European Central Bank (ECB); increased coordination of monetary policies through the EMI (although responsibility for the conduct of monetary policy remained the privilege of the national authorities); the establishment of full independence for the national central banks; and further preparatory work for Stage Three.
3. Stage Three, to become effective on January 1, 1999, would be characterized by the irrevocable fixing of exchange rates, the introduction of the single currency,[78] and transfer of responsibility for the single monetary policy to the European Central Bank (ECB).

The treaty specified convergence criteria, which clearly showed that the Germans had made few concessions on their views of how a monetary order should be made up: If political union was not possible, then well-defined limits on economic and budgetary policies would create a de facto political union. Entry into the monetary union was only possible for those countries that fulfilled the hotly debated convergence criteria:

- an inflation rate not more than 1.5 percent higher than the average of the three lowest inflation rates among the candidate members
- a long-term interest rate not more than 2 percent higher than the average observed in the three low-inflation countries
- member of the exchange rate mechanism of the EMS and not experience a devaluation during the two years preceding entrance into the union
- a government budget deficit not higher than 3 percent of GDP; the deficit should be declining continuously and substantially and come close to the 3 percent norm, or alternatively, the deviation from 3 percent should be exceptional and temporary and should remain close to 3 percent
- a government debt not exceeding 60 percent of GDP (if a country is above 60 percent, its government debt should diminish sufficiently and approach 60 percent at a satisfactory pace)

Two other stipulations of the Maastricht Treaty would prove important in later years. First, national central banks or the ECB were not allowed to finance government budget deficits of any kind directly. Second, the treaty stipulated a no bailout clause: Neither the EC in general nor any individual member of the EMU could be held liable for the financial commitments of any other member.

Given all these conditions and requirements, the claim by Germany's finance minister, Theo Waigel, that the "treaty on economic and monetary union, agreed after long and intense negotiations, bears the German hallmark; our stability policy has become the leitmotif for the future monetary order"[79] seemed very true—at least on paper and for the time being.

The belief in the stability of the Basel-Nyborg consensus and the unusual swiftness (considering the usual length of deliberations in the EC) of the move toward the Maastricht Treaty impressed the markets—so much so that a belief that the EMS parities were fixed began to dominate market psychology. Entry into the ERM by Spain in June 1989, Great Britain in October 1990, and Portugal in April 1992 further reinforced that attitude. All three of these countries opted for the wider fluctuation margin of +/− 6 percent, whereas Italy changed in early 1989 to the smaller fluctuation margin of +/− 2.25 percent.

Daniel Gros and Niels Thygesen, two of the most respected European specialists on monetary union, concluded in 1992 that "overall, there is…little reason to believe that the EMS would be destabilized by random self-fulfilling attacks in the 1990s."[80] Indeed, instead of a random self-fulfilling attack on the EMS, a largely nonrandom crisis blew the EMS to pieces by August 1993.

The EMS Undermined

The aftermath of the German reunification was the first of four elements that lay at the origin of the crisis within the EMS and the ERM. The German government's economic and monetary management of reunification produced much tension within the EMS, as reunification led to substantial and persistent budget deficits for the German government. Huge transfers flowed from the rich West to the poor East. The one-for-one exchange rate established between the West German mark and the East German mark created an increase in the money supply unmatched by production in the real economy. To avoid escalating inflation due to the demand stimulus, the Bundesbank deemed it necessary to follow a restrictive monetary policy that produced high interest rates.

Upward pressure on the D-mark followed from the combination of expansionary budgetary policy with a restrictive monetary policy. The other members of the EMS faced a simple choice: Either try to maintain the parity between their currency and the D-mark and subject themselves to high interest rates, or let their currencies devalue against the D-mark in order to escape the high rates.[81]

Until the summer of 1992, Germany's EMS partners chose the first option, which weighed heavily on economic activity outside Germany. Unemployment rates increased to more than 10 percent in France and Great Britain. Markets sensed that, politically speaking, Bundesbank policies had become untenable for most of the other EMS members.

The unwinding of what the International Monetary Fund (IMF) termed the "convergence play" was the second element feeding the EMS crisis.[82] (In twenty-first-century parlance, the phenomenon is known as "carry trade.") This convergence play was based in the belief that the exchange rates were truly fixed. Such a belief gave rise to risk-free profit opportunities, whereby investors borrowed in low-interest-rate countries and re-invested in higher-interest-rate countries (and so, as the theory goes, bringing about "convergence" in interest rates).

In 1990, for example, German short-term interest rates averaged 8.5 percent, compared to 10.3 percent in France, 12.2 percent in Italy, 14.8 percent in Great Britain, and 15.2 percent in Spain. The IMF estimated that until the spring of 1992, at least $300 billion was circulating in this convergence play.[83] Needless to say, the supposedly risk-free characteristics of this arbitraging disappeared once belief in firmly fixed exchange rates started to dwindle. Moreover, as the positions taken in this convergence play unwound, the currencies involved had a greater tendency toward revaluation and devaluation.

The Maastricht Treaty itself was the third destabilizing factor. The ratification of the Treaty was accompanied by political uncertainty. In June 1992, Danish voters rejected the Maastricht Treaty. Jean-Claude Trichet, who was then the director of the French treasury and later president of the European Central Bank, commented that "Denmark should be punished for its foolishness."[84] Wolfgang Rieke, head of the Bundesbank's international department, described the Danish rejection as "a well-timed reminder."[85]

In September 1992, the French accepted the Treaty by the smallest of margins (the famous *"petit oui"* or "small yes"). The Treaty's criterion that a country must be devaluation-free for at least two years to be allowed into the monetary union also increased uncertainty. Fears became widespread that some countries would try to gain competitive advantage by devaluating their currency before the start of the two-year deadline. Again, expectations of such realignments made them more likely to occur.

The attitude of the top leaders of the Bundesbank, who embodied what David Marsh described as the "sheer persistence and occasional brutality of German economic officialdom," made up the fourth and final factor.[86] The powerful bank showed again and again that its priority was monetary management of the German economy. Arguments from the French and other European leaders for a more relaxed German monetary policy did little to sway the Bundesbank's leaders, who were known for stubbornly defending its positions. As Wim Duisenberg, the Dutchman who would become the ECB's first president, once said: "The Bundesbank is like whipped cream. The harder you beat it, the stiffer it gets."[87]

The Buba had long had a stubborn attitude for three main reasons. First, its leaders had long believed that EMU was destined to fail. In January 1991, Bundesbank President Karl Otto Pöhl warned the European Parliament that the currency union would be "a disaster," thus conveying the message that Germany would probably not participate in EMU.[88] Second, the Buba was convinced that its monetary policy was best and required no adjustments whatsoever. Third, the technocrats of the Buba knew that the German public respected them more than they respected the politicians. As Jacques Delors once said, "Not all Germans believe in God, but all believe in the Bundesbank."[89] The markets concluded that, given the public's support of the Buba's stubbornness and the increasing tensions within the EMS, the "others" in the exchange rate mechanism would have to throw in the towel. And so it happened.

Implosion of the EMS

In June 1992, the Bundesbank hiked its policy interest rate from 8 percent to 8.75 percent, bringing tensions within the EMS to a boiling point. Massive central bank interventions could no longer keep currencies within the EMS fluctuation margins.[90] In September 1992, the system went into cardiac arrest. First, the Italian lira was devalued, and then the British took the pound sterling out of the ERM.[91] Next, the Spanish peseta was devalued by 5 percent, and the lira was taken out of the ERM.

Speculation against the French franc was countered by massive support interventions. This led to bickering between the French, who wanted the Germans to be more supportive, and the Germans (especially top officials at the Buba), who felt they were already too supportive of the franc. Bundesbank president Helmut Schlesinger described central bank interventions to support weak currencies as "a powerful incentive for speculation."[92] The very principled career Bundesbanker Schlesinger had taken over from Pöhl, who had resigned in May 1991 over a disagreement with the government's policy on the financing of German reunification.

The storm calmed, but in the summer of 1993, the pressure on the French franc intensified. The debate over how to save the EMS grew heated, with the collective political world of France and Germany going against the leaders of the Bundesbank. Schlesinger went as far as publicly opposing German Finance Minister Waigel. The question was no longer if the EMS would explode, but when.

The French wanted the Germans to leave the EMS, in the hopes that doing so would pave the way for the franc to anchor the EMS. But when Belgium and the Netherlands declared that they would leave with Germany, the French backtracked. They feared such movements would decrease France's prestige and cement Germany's dominance.

Following a proposal by Banque de France Governor Jacques de Larosière, the fluctuation margins within the EMS were broadened drastically, to +/– 15 percent, on August 2, 1993. The original concept of the EMS was blown to pieces. Shortly afterward, Schlesinger was replaced as Bundesbank president by his deputy, Hans Tietmeyer, who was thought (incorrectly, as it turned out) to be more receptive to the agenda of the Kohl government.

Within weeks, the Buba relaxed its monetary policy. After falling from 8.75 percent in August 1992 to 6.75 percent in August 1993, the main rate stood at 4.50 percent by May 1994 and at 3.50 percent by August 1995—lending some credence to the argument that Bundesbank strategists had been playing hardball. Relative calm returned to what remained of the EMS, mostly because the other countries cautiously followed the interest rate declines of the Bundesbank.

The Spanish and Portuguese devaluations of March 1995 did not produce additional tensions, although Yves-Thibault de Silguy, the Frenchman responsible for economic and monetary affairs within the European Commission, used the occasion to warn that "if the single currency does not arrive, the very existence of the single market would be threatened."[93] In January 1995, the Austrian krona joined the EMS; the Finnish markka followed in October 1996. In November 1996 the Italian lira rejoined—just in the nick of time, given the requirement to be devaluation-free for two years before the EMU start date of January 1, 1999.

Maastricht Voodoo

As the January 1, 1999 start date approached, the Maastricht criteria on budget deficits and government debts led to heated debates

and data manipulation of all sorts. Most EMU candidates produced data that indicated sufficient conformity with the criteria.
Countries wanting to join the EMU could not have a budget deficit exceeding 3 percent of GDP, and their government debt could
not exceed 60 percent—with the important caveat that countries
not fulfilling these criteria must be approaching the desired levels.[94]

At the time the Maastricht Treaty was signed, many countries
that wanted to join the EMU did not meet the deficit and debt
criteria. At the end of 1993, Belgium's government debt was 141
percent of GDP and Italy's was 116 percent. The number of countries with budget deficits in excess of 3 percent was impressive.
Italy's 1993 deficit stood at 10 percent of GDP, Finland's at 8 percent, Belgium's and Spain's at 7 percent, and France's at 6 percent.[95]
Since the criteria were so far out of reach for these countries, the
political machinery went into overdrive. While several countries
took on genuine policy initiatives to cut budget deficits, others
took aim at artificially lowering budget deficits.

Sometimes the debate about exactly what "approaching" a
deficit of 3 percent or a debt level of 60 percent meant became
truly hilarious. Fons Verplaetse, then governor of Belgium's central
bank, argued with a straight face that a deficit of 3.999 percent
was equivalent to one of 3 percent. Government ministers nodded
in agreement. These interventions and discussions reached a high
point with the 1997 budgets, because that year's data was the basis
for deciding which countries would be allowed to join the EMU.

Nearly every country aiming for acceptance into the EMU applied statistical manipulation and creative accounting. These tricks
included:

- keeping expenses out of the books
- selling government assets and booking them as recurrent
  receipts

- blatant exaggeration of expected income from the fight against fiscal and social fraud
- announcing savings in expenditures that would never be executed and tax increases that would never become truly effective
- ingenious manipulation of data on nominal GDP so as to make deficits and debt levels look smaller as a percent of GDP

Although Italy, Greece, Spain, and Belgium topped the list of suspects, even the German government tried to bend the rules by taking advantage of the Bundesbank's stock of gold.[96] The French government proposed to use funds in the pension system of the giant telecommunications company France Telecom to reduce its budget deficits—a trick the Belgian government would also try later. The European Commission had to control the budgeting process, but political necessities and considerations would clearly always prevail over economic and monetary orthodoxy. Not surprisingly, the commission's protests against this budgetary hocus pocus were anything but explicit or forceful.

In the meantime, EMU decision making continued. In October 1993, it was decided to locate the EMI, the forerunner of the ECB, in Frankfurt, hometown of the Bundesbank—as the Germans wanted to ensure that the ECB was clearly identified with the Bundesbank. In an attempt to weaken that connection, the French and their allies proposed locating the EMI in Bonn, the former capital of West Germany, but Kohl rejected all alternatives to Frankfurt. Mitterrand explained to his prime minister Édouard Balladur that the acceptance of Frankfurt was "necessary to get the Germans to accept the end of the D-mark, to allay their anxieties."[97]

Hungarian-born Belgian Alexandre Lamfalussy, general manager at the Bank for International Settlements in Basel, Switzerland, was chosen to run the EMI. A seasoned monetary technocrat fluent in German, French, and English, Lamfalussy was considered shrewd enough to bridge the different opinions about how to get the ECB up and running. More specifically, he needed to reconcile the German desire for a politically independent central bank and the French desire for direct political supervision of the single monetary policy under EMU.

One of the first issues on Lamfalussy's plate was the question of the financial market activities of the ECB. The French wanted these activities to be carried out by the trading desks of the national central banks—mainly in order to prevent the boost Frankfurt would get (to the detriment of Paris) from centralization of these activities. But the Germans carried the day, and a central dealing room was installed at the EMI in Frankfurt.

To Delay or Not

In 1994, discussions about which countries would join the EMU from its start (on January 1, 1999) became even hotter. Germany and its major ally, the Netherlands, advocated for a core group of countries to form the starting group: Germany, France, and the Benelux countries (despite Belgium's very high government debt).[98] Italy and Spain protested this proposal.

In his 1995 campaign for the French presidency, Jacques Chirac expressed doubt that the EMU timetable was realistic. Afraid of being left out, Italian Prime Minister Lamberto Dini also pleaded in September 1995 for delay of the third and final stage by two or three years. In Germany, Otmar Issing warned in 1996 that the timing of the whole project was wrong: "The whole strategy to use the monetary union as a way to get to political union is putting the cart before the horse."[99] In September 1997, the Bundesbank's president, Hans Tietmeyer, declared that the "heavens would not fall in" if the start of the monetary union was delayed.[100]

Within Europe, opposition to monetary union was sharpest

in Germany. In February 1998, 155 German university professors wrote a public letter arguing strongly for the postponement of the EMU's start. A few weeks earlier, four German professors—constitutional law expert Karl Albrecht Schachtschneider and economists Wilhelm Hankel, Joachim Starbatty, and Wilhelm Nölling—had waged a 352-page complaint against EMU at the German Federal Constitutional Court, arguing that its stipulations were unconstitutional.[101] Former German Chancellor Helmut Schmidt described this gang of four as "idiots savants with no sense of history."[102] In March 1998, the newly elected German chancellor, Gerhard Schröder, described the euro as "a premature sickly child."[103] The late 1990s also saw a tsunami of analyses—mainly from American economists—concluding that the EMU as conceived was likely a mistake.

In February 1997, the major central bankers of the world met at Basel's Bank for International Settlements (BIS). The meeting quickly turned into a heated discussion about delaying in the start of EMU.[104] To the consternation of the other Europeans present, Wim Duisenberg, who at that time was president of the BIS and the Dutch central bank (de Nederlandsche Bank), agreed with the delay proposal laid out by Eddie George, governor of the Bank of England. Duisenberg was already in the running to become the first president of the ECB.[105] Noting the Germans' hesitation, Jean-Claude Trichet, at that time governor of the Banque de France, declared that a delay would be both ridiculous and dangerous. In an interview with *Le Monde*, Valéry Giscard d'Estaing stated very explicitly that if monetary union did not go ahead as planned, "that will be a very dangerous situation for France...(that) would be the end of a long period of Franco-German organisation of Europe, and the transition to a preponderant influence by Germany."[106]

Debate over the principles that would guide policy in the

member countries complicated the discussion of which countries would initially be included. Quite predictably, this debate pitted Germany and the Netherlands against France, Italy, and the other like-minded Southern European countries.

At the December 1995 European summit meeting in Madrid, European leaders agreed on Waigel's broad plan for the Stability Pact. This was also the summit at which the European leaders decided not only on *euro* as the name of the EMU's single currency but also on the definitive timetable for launching the project. On January 1, 1999, the exchange rates of the currencies of the EMU member states would be irrevocably locked. Three years later, euro notes and coins would be put into circulation in all participating member states, replacing the national currencies.

The basic element of Waigel's Stability Pact was that member countries would be fined for budget deficits larger than 3 percent of GDP. During the December 1996 European summit in Dublin, Helmut Kohl and Jacques Chirac clashed over the content of the Stability Pact. After a tense and bitter argument, the pact was renamed the Stability and Growth Pact (SGP). Although the basic ingredients remained, the pact's disciplinary effect was substantially weakened. Almost immediately, economists warned of the impracticality of imposing fines on democratically elected governments.[107]

Many years later, Charles Wyplosz, professor of international economics at the Graduate Institute in Geneva and a specialist on the EMU, described the SGP as the third safeguard for the whole system, after the bailout clause and barring the ECB from directly financing public debts. At the time of the euro's birth, Wyplosz argues, "it was clear that monetary union would not deliver price stability unless fiscal discipline was guaranteed. Perfectly aware of this original sin, the authors of the Maastricht Treaty introduced no less than three safeguards."[108] But the euro crisis that started in the fall of 2009 made this set of safeguards look like a house of cards.

In the months after the Dublin summit, the French booked another small victory over the Germans in the management of the monetary union. It was agreed that a eurogroup of finance ministers would meet regularly with the ECB to discuss policy matters. The installation of this group gave the French some political influence over the ECB's decision making. The tenacity of the French on this issue was clearly demonstrated by a statement of their prime minister, Michel Rocard: "Independence of the Central Bank is a means to an end, to win Germany's approval for the monetary union, but it is not the end of the story."[109] The impact of this eurogroup on monetary policy was marginal at best.

Tumultuous Last Line, Fine Start

It was also decided at the Dublin summit that Wim Duisenberg would take over from Alexandre Lamfalussy as head of the EMI Council. Duisenberg had been put forward as a candidate in June 1996. Immediately, a new clash developed between the French and the Germans. The Germans felt that Duisenberg was the obvious choice for first president of the ECB. The French thought it outrageous that the central bankers themselves would select the ECB's first boss.

Chirac put forward Jean-Claude Trichet, governor of the Banque de France, as his candidate. Trichet and Chirac were not exactly good friends—they had clashed frequently over Trichet's *franc fort* policy[110]—but the French president saw no other option after the Germans torpedoed the candidacy of Michel Camdessus, the Frenchman who in those days led the IMF and not exactly to the Germans' liking.

The discussion dragged on for months, becoming increasingly heated. Toward the end of 1997, Helmut Hesse, a member of the Bundesbank Directorate, declared in a French newspaper, "One thing is certain: The first president of the ECB will not be

a Frenchman."[111] In April 1998, Bundesbank president Hans Tietmeyer openly expressed his support of Duisenberg.[112]

The discussion came to a head during the May 1998 European summit in Brussels. Summit chairman Tony Blair, the British
prime minister, described the discussions as a messy negotiation
where French pride ran into Dutch obstinacy and collided with
German interests.[113] The arguments between Chirac and Dutch
Prime Minister Wim Kok became quite vicious; in fact, Austrian
Chancellor Viktor Klima remarked that he had never witnessed
such a fight before during his political life.[114]

Still very displeased with the candidacy of Duisenberg, whom
the French considered quasi-German, Chirac insisted that Duisenberg leave the job early in July 2002. On May, 2, 1998, it was announced officially that Duisenberg would be the first president of
the ECB, with Christian Noyer of the French treasury as deputy
president. During the press conference following the Brussels summit, Chirac claimed that Duisenberg had insisted he would leave
the job early; subsequently, the assembled international press burst
into laughter. When a furious Chirac tried to counter, the laughter
only became louder. A few days later, Duisenberg told the European
Parliament that he would probably serve the full eight-year term.
Relations between Chirac and Duisenberg never normalized.

Several official reports during the spring of 1998 concluded
that eleven countries met the convergence criteria as stipulated
in the Maastricht Treaty.[115] However, on the basis of 1998 data,
only four EU members—Denmark, the UK, Luxembourg, and
France—fulfilled the conditions in the strict sense, and only the last
two were prepared to join the monetary union. The starting members also included Italy, a country whose participation was strongly
contested. According to Nout Wellink, Duisenberg's successor as
president of the Dutch central bank, Duisenberg told him in 1997
that "we will get EMU from 1 January 1999, and whatever hap-

pens, Italy will be part of it." Wellink added, "Italy was a founding member of the European Community. These people know how to construct the figures (on Italy's economic performance) to satisfy the convergence criteria."[116]

On June 1, 1998, the EMI transformed into the ECB. Literally overnight, the ECB became the second most important central bank of the world, and certainly one of the most independent ones. The U.S. Congress has the power to change the statutes of the Federal Reserve, for example, but neither the European Parliament nor the national parliaments of the EMU member countries have formal powers over the ECB. The major decision-making bodies of the ECB are the executive board, consisting of the ECB president and five other members, and the governing council, in which the members of the executive board are joined by the governors of the national central banks of the EMU members. Each member of the executive board serves a nonrenewable term of seven years.

A few months after the ECB's formal start, the governing council clarified its overriding objective of maintaining price stability: the ECB wanted to keep the consumer price inflation index for the whole euro area "below 2 percent over the medium term." This objective was criticized as too restrictive and asymmetric, since it did not sufficiently take into account the possibility of potential deflationary developments and their consequences for monetary policy. In 2003, the ECB responded to this criticism by changing its policy objective with respect to price stability as "below, but close to, 2 percent."

On January 1, 1999, the EMU became reality, although the euro existed only as a unit of account. The starting group consisted of Austria, Belgium, Finland, France, Germany, Italy, Ireland, Luxembourg, the Netherlands, Portugal, and Spain. Greece joined the euro club in 2001, followed by Slovenia in 2007, Cyprus and Malta in 2008, Slovakia in 2009, and Estonia in 2011. David Marsh described this radical change in Europe's economic and monetary landscape as a "bloodless, noiseless, bureaucratic revolution. But it was a revolution all the same: an unprecedented, self-willed abrogation of state prerogative."[117]

On January 1, 2002, the national currencies of the EMU members were replaced by the euro. The transition was remarkably smooth. On November 1, 2003, Jean-Claude Trichet succeeded Duisenberg as president of the ECB.[118] By then, the euro was firmly established. The EMU, it seemed, was well on its way to becoming an indisputable success, and the Cassandras who had predicted the self-destruction of the whole enterprise were ignored and sometimes even openly ridiculed.

The next chapter contrasts the general optimism about the EMU and the euro with the results of economic research on the requirements for a durable and efficient monetary union. Applying the optimum currency theory to the setup of EMU led to much more sobering, if not outright pessimistic, conclusions about its future.

Chapter 2

Unfinished business

THE TWIN LAUNCHES OF THE EMU AND THE EURO were lauded throughout Europe as a step toward true unity and an end to centuries of conflict on the continent. The atmosphere was euphoric. It was considered politically incorrect to even to criticize the project. In the words of Paul Krugman,

> political leaders throughout Europe were caught up in the romance of the project, to such an extent that anyone who expressed scepticism was considered outside the mainstream.... [The creation of the euro]... was supposed to be the finest moment in a grand and noble undertaking: the generations-long effort to bring peace, democracy, and shared prosperity to a once and frequently war-torn continent.[119]

But was all this optimism warranted? Would the monetary union function smoothly and efficiently? Would it bring about the peaceful unification of which so many in Europe dreamed?

As the EMU project gathered steam in the 1990s, politicians tended to present monetary union as no less than manna from heaven. In some countries, such overselling was the only way to gain the people's support. Many American economists contested this optimistic view.[120] Perhaps the most striking thing about the

American criticism was that it came from all over the ideological spectrum. Right-wing monetarist Milton Friedman considered it "highly unlikely that [the euro] is going to be a great success."[121] The more left-wing Keynesian Franco Modigliani pointed to "the difficulties in a system which will have fixed exchange rates" and the requirement for "a great deal of flexibility in the behavior of wages of individual countries having differential productivity growth and facing external shocks."[122]

German-born philosopher and sociologist Ralf Dahrendorf was among the few European critics. He wrote in early 1998,

> Pretty soon the people of Europe will realise that the great promises with which their leaders have sold them the project will not come true. Growth will be dependent on the same old internal and external factors, and Asia will be more important for them than EMU.[123]

Several years earlier, the famous report *One Market, One Money* argued that the benefits of monetary union would outweigh its costs. The objectivity of this and related reports remains questionable. My own off-the-record conversations with several individuals involved with those reports confirm the story told by Krugman:

> Back in the '90s, people who were present [in the making of the euro project] told me that staff members at the European Commission were initially instructed to prepare reports on the costs and the benefits of a single currency—but after their superiors got a look at some preliminary work, those instructions were altered: they were told to prepare reports just on the benefits. To be fair, when I've told that story to others who were senior officials at that time, they've disputed that—but whoever's version is right, the fact that some people were making such a claim captures the spirit of the time.[124]

To better understand the arguments for and against monetary union, one must analyze the advantages and disadvantages in a coherent framework. The theory of optimum currency areas offers such a framework.

Multiple Benefits

Several advantages of monetary union are undeniable.[125] For example, the absence of currency conversion costs contributes to economic efficiency. Greater price transparency across countries helps the competitive process and lowers prices, keeping inflation in check and interest rates low. Integration of financial markets makes financial intermediation and investment processes more efficient. These advantages contribute to the development of economic activity. The political independence of the ECB and its focus on price stability reduce uncertainty for all economic agents.

With a single currency, exchange rate risks cease to exist in the union area. This reduces uncertainty and stimulates trade, investment, and economic activity in general. The single currency bans competitive devaluations, reducing trade tensions and protectionist inclinations in the common market for goods and services. Wild fluctuations in currency exchange rates had contributed to the devastating economic and political disruptions of the 1920s and 1930s. A monetary union was a step away from the conflicts of the past.

In the earlier phases of the monetary union, countries that suffered from chronic inflation and stability problems reaped great benefits from joining, particularly in the form of lower interest rates. They essentially gained the low-inflation credibility of Germany, the EMU's anchor country.[126] However, overexpansion in interest rate–sensitive sectors of the economy created major disequilibria. In addition, lower interest rates made governments less careful about budget deficits and increases in outstanding debt. These themes will return in Chapter 3.

Another advantage became obvious during the financial crisis of 2007 to 2009. Smaller member countries, especially those with major banking sectors, better withstood the crisis thanks to the protective umbrella of the larger eurozone. Although Denmark was not a member of the monetary union, Nils Bernstein, governor of the Danish central bank, acknowledged that "there are big advantages during a crisis to be inside [the eurozone] and much more protected against turmoil and to have access to the euro system's facilities."[127]

The crisis led to an exchange rate collapse for smaller non-EMU countries, such as Iceland and Hungary, and exacerbated the meltdown of their banking sectors. Eurozone membership avoided such extreme hardship in the short run but also created a false sense of security among policymakers. Nonmember countries, like Iceland, had to face the crisis head on. On the other hand, the recoveries of countries such as Iceland were aided by the freedom they had to let their currency devalue.

The Dollar and All That

Perhaps one of the strongest arguments in favor of the EMU was that the single currency made member states less dependent on the wild fluctuations of the dollar, still the dominant currency worldwide. The population and economic weight of the eurozone positioned the euro to equal the dollar in the international economic and financial arena.

A strongly rising dollar, for example, pushes up European prices for energy and raw materials (most of which are priced in dollars), fuels inflation, and forces central banks to switch to a more restrictive, growth-unfriendly monetary policy. A rapidly declining dollar created serious competition problems for major European export industries.

European policymakers were most frustrated by the American authorities' unreceptiveness to complaints from Europe about the dollar's gyrations. John Connally, who served as secretary of the treasury under Richard Nixon, told European leaders complaining about the dollar's freefall in 1973–74 that "the dollar is our currency and your problem."

The monetary union had been created not only for reasons of financial tranquility and economic efficiency, but also for geopolitical reasons. European politicians were determined to prevent a repetition of the devastating world wars the European continent had suffered. A peaceful Europe could only be achieved if Germany and France put aside their historical antagonism. EMU and the euro were the vehicles chosen to achieve that laudable goal.

The "German problem" was very real to those countries that had endured German aggression. The French concluded that the solution was to unify the continent, encapsulating Germany within a greater political body. German politicians, humiliated by the devastation their nation had caused during World War II, were equally anxious to avoid future conflict. On the occasion of his eightieth birthday in May 2010, Helmut Kohl told a German audience, "Today, I'm convinced more than ever that European unification is a question of war and peace for Europe and for us, and the euro is part of our guarantee of peace."[128]

Unfortunately, political considerations eclipsed the monetary and economic issues. In the words of Howard Davies and David Green, "The political motive was so powerful that it may have blinded some of the founding fathers to what the commitment to a single currency involved in practice."[129] Contrast this argument with the one made by Jacques Delors: "Obsession about budgetary constraints means that the people forget too often about the political objectives of European construction. The argument in favour of the single currency should be based on the desire to live together in peace."[130]

One Size Seldom Fits All

While the advantages of monetary union are real, quantifying these advantages is another story. The prevention of war between member countries is certainly a major achievement. The question is how much credit, if any, the monetary union deserves for preserving peace. Leading American economist Martin Feldstein predicted several years before the start of the EMU that instead of preventing war between European countries, the monetary union would make war.[131] Obviously, this hasn't happened yet.

But the economic, political, and other benefits of monetary union are based on the assumption that the union functions smoothly and efficiently. Lower transaction costs, greater price transparency, stable exchange rates, and more integrated financial systems have little value without financial and economic stability. At the end of the day, the long-term viability of the monetary union depends on whether the union's institutional environment is strong enough to prevent degeneration into major financial instability.

The major disadvantage of joining a monetary union is the loss of an independent monetary policy. When it comes to monetary policy, one size may not fit all. The union's monetary policy may be too tight for the economy of one member country and too loose for another. Of course, the chosen policy might not be too different from a country's optimal policy. Significant deviation, however, may lead to higher inflation, increases in unemployment, and escalating deficits.

A country's loss of power over monetary policy has important consequences. It is in a monetary union's best interest to correct imbalances in the economies of member countries as quickly as possible. The first approach should be to let market forces correct the imbalances. When this solution is insufficient—for example because regulation or powerful interest groups stand in the way—

national authorities of the countries in question should exercise nonmonetary policy levers. During the first decade of the euro's existence, such considerations sounded rather theoretical to politicians. By 2009, they had become all too real.

The loss of the variable exchange rate as an economic policy tool is yet another related disadvantage. When a country's internal costs rise disproportionately with international costs, variable exchange rates give the country the option of devaluing its currency to remain competitive. Similarly, when a country is hit by an asymmetric shock, an exchange rate adjustment can aid recovery.[132]

A Look at Belgium

Belgium, one of the founding members of the EMU, is a country with a small and open economy. It serves as an excellent illustration of how the disadvantages of a monetary union can affect an individual country.

At the end of 1981, Belgium faced a severe social and economic crisis. Unemployment rose fast. The trade balance went from bad to worse, and the budget followed. The exchange rate of the Belgian franc versus the D-mark could only be maintained through regular interventions in the currency markets that depleted the country's international reserves, and through very high interest rates. This created a vicious cycle that brought Belgium to its knees.

Leaders of Belgium's central bank, the Nationale Bank van België (NBB), met in late 1981 with representatives of major socioeconomic organizations. NBB chief economist Roland Beauvois argued that Belgium's two largest problems were a loss of international competitiveness due to the rise in wage costs and a rapidly increasing budget deficit. To tackle these problems, Beauvois suggested asking all Belgians to give up 10 percent of their gross wages—5 percent to be retained by the employer to reduce labor costs and 5 percent to transfer to the government to reduce the budget deficit. Georges Debunne, leader of the socialist labor union, declared that he would "put the country on fire" if this policy were implemented. NBB governor Cecil de Strycker, well aware that the Belgian government could not withstand strikes and street demonstrations, responded, *"Alors, messieurs, il n'y a que la devaluation"* ("Well, gentlemen, devaluation is then the only policy option that remains").

Before the end of 1981, the NBB had always rejected the option of devaluation. The extreme openness of the Belgian economy meant a devaluation would immediately push up import prices and increase the consumer price index, and direct wage indexation would lead to new wage increases and inflation. Corporations would be bankrupted, jobs would be destroyed, and the government budget would descend further into deficit. The NBB warned that, if no additional measures were taken to correct economic imbalances, devaluation would only be a temporary fix. The bank doubted the Belgian government would have the stomach to push those additional measures through. Lacking other options and under considerable pressure from the IMF, the NBB devalued the Belgian franc within the EMS by 8.5 percent in February 1982.

The NBB's major mistake was underestimating the shock effect devaluation would have. Contrary to expectations, devaluation opened the door to policy measures that had previously been unthinkable. The direct wage indexation mechanism was suspended. Savings in the social security system were pushed through to reduce the budget deficit. Tax measures were undertaken to stimulate risk taking and entrepreneurship. The devaluation improved the international competitiveness of Belgian companies overnight, increasing net exports. As a result, external demand largely compensated for the fall in internal demand caused by the expenditure cuts and tax increases. The Belgian economy experienced a prolonged period of relatively good performance.

What's the moral of Belgium's story? For countries outside a monetary union, the freedom to pursue an independent monetary policy can be quite valuable when the economy falls into crisis-disequilibrium. A currency devaluation makes sense when, for example, labor costs are disproportionate with those of competing countries, or in the case of asymmetric shocks. Not only will a devaluation immediately bring those costs in line, but as the Belgian example shows, the shock effect can open up new policy options.[133]

Member countries of a currency or monetary union, lacking the option of devaluation, have only one policy option for solving problems of this kind: internal deflation, which is a direct, nominal decrease of internal (especially labor) costs. However, this deflationary process is difficult to implement, especially in democratic countries, where powerful interest groups may offer fierce resistance. Given the limitations placed on the available policy options, the best choice for countries belonging to a monetary union is to prevent major disequilibria from happening in the first place.

The Checklist

A monetary union can be defined as successful if, for every member country, the benefits of belonging to the union outweigh the costs associated with the loss of policy tools. The literature on the economic theory of optimum currency area (OCA) provides a list of eight elements needed for a smoothly functioning monetary union.[134]

1. *Mobility of factors of production, especially labor.* This need formed the cornerstone of Robert Mundell's seminal contribution to the OCA theory.[135] The greater this mobility, the better the economic system will adjust to asymmetric shocks, and the smaller the cost associated with the loss of an independent monetary policy.

2. *Price and wage flexibility.* Max Corden, an eminent scholar in monetary affairs, emphasizes price and wage flexibility.[136]

Such flexibility helps to prevent inflationary differentials, cost disadvantages, and unemployment.

3. *Similar inflation rates.* When inflation rates between countries remain low and similar over time, the terms of trade between these countries will also be fairly stable, reducing the need for nominal exchange rate adjustments.[137] Differences in inflation rates inevitably result in cost disadvantages for higher-inflation countries.

4. *Degree of openness of the individual economies.* The more open an economy, the less useful an exchange rate adjustment becomes for correcting asymmetric shocks or cost disadvantages. Hence, the more open an economy, the smaller the disadvantages of joining a monetary union.[138]

5. *Degree of diversification of the individual economies.* Countries with more diverse economies are less vulnerable to shocks to specific sectors of the economy and will feel the effects of asymmetric shocks to a lesser degree. More diversified economies are less likely to need to adjust their exchange rate.[139]

6. *Financial integration.* When the financial markets of a union's member countries are well integrated, small differences in interest rates will bring about capital flows to cushion the adjustment to adverse disturbances. Financial integration can also reduce the need for exchange rate adjustments.[140] Robert Mundell argued that financial integration contributes to the stability of a currency area through cross-country asset holdings and pooling of foreign exchange reserves, which can help mitigate the effects of asymmetric shocks.[141]

7. *Fiscal integration.* Monetary unions need transparent fiscal transfer mechanisms to redistribute funds in order to be able to adjust to asymmetric shocks as smoothly as possible.

Fiscal integration also reduces the need for independent monetary policies and exchange rate adjustments.[142]

8. *Political integration.* The political will to integrate "fosters compliance with joint commitments, sustains cooperation on various economic policies and encourages more institutional linkages."[143] Austrian economist Gottfried Haberler stressed the importance of similar policy attitudes and convictions among member countries.[144] Political integration obviously helps to bring about policy convergence that leads to convergence in economic development (reducing the need to fall back on autonomous monetary policies).

Fulfillment of these eight conditions will synchronize the business cycle throughout the monetary union. If the cycle is well synchronized, the need for nation-specific macroeconomic policies will be reduced. However, even when different members of a highly synchronized monetary union experience identical shocks, their ideal policy responses may differ due to, for example, the countries' initial economic positions, tax structures, trade responsiveness, and national preferences.[145]

The OCA theory's view of the EMU was widely misunderstood from the beginning. It was, for example, simply not true, as some claimed, that "OCA theory predicted in the first place that the euro would never happen."[146] It certainly predicted that if the conditions were not satisfied, the monetary union would not function optimally. Discrepancies between reality and the theoretical optimum would lead to proportional economic costs for member countries and increase the chance that the union would eventually break up.

The Red Flag That Stayed Down

It is difficult to argue that the original eleven EMU member countries met all of the OCA conditions. Mobility of labor, flexibility of wages and prices, fiscal integration, and political integration were met weakly, if at all. The EMU was more successful in satisfying the conditions of similar inflation rates, degree of openness, degree of diversification, and financial integration. On the whole, if the EMU decision makers had given serious consideration to OCA theory, red flags should have been raised during the 1990s.

David Archer, assistant governor of the Reserve Bank of New Zealand, captured the atmosphere surrounding the discussion on monetary union and OCA criteria when he argued that one should not accept too readily that

> EMU had something to do with the theory of optimal currency areas. On the few occasions that I was present at pre-EMU conferences where the prospect of EMU was under discussion, only the Anglo-Saxon (mainly North American) economists present were approaching the issue from the perspective of optimal currency analysis. The European economists present either recognised the paramount place of political motivations, or focused on other facets of the economic analysis.[147]

Europe's decision to ignore American criticism was as complete as it was remarkable. American economists were comparing their own single-currency union with the EMU.[148] The United States, after all, can be considered "the world's most successful single currency union."[149] "America," wrote Paul Krugman, "has a currency union that works, and we know why it works: because it coincides with a nation—a nation with a big government, a common language, and a shared culture. Europe has none of these things."[150]

The American federation uses a system of fiscal transfers with clear and unambiguous rules to correct imbalances.[151] Xavier Sala-i-Martin and Jeffrey Sachs calculated that fiscal transfers within the United States eliminate up to 40 percent of a decline in regional income.[152]

Moreover, the United States had significant mobility of labor and capital long before it became a monetary union,[153] and its labor markets and wages are still less rigid than those of EMU members. Whereas less than 0.1 percent of the eurozone population moves permanently from one eurozone country to another, the comparable figure for movement among U.S. states is 2.5 percent.[154] Labor mobility is up to three times higher in the United States than in Europe.[155]

The U.S. monetary union is much better equipped than the EMU to deal with asymmetric shocks. In the United States, a regional economic shock is largely absorbed by the outflow of workers to other regions, while the result of such shocks in Europe is increased unemployment.[156]

One major difference between the experiences of the United States and Europe is the timing of bringing about a political and monetary union. In the United States, political union preceded monetary union by several decades. In Europe, monetary union was, in the eyes of many, created as a means to political union. Duisenberg, the first president of the ECB, declared that "EMU is, and was always meant to be a stepping stone on the way to a united Europe."[157] This attitude may have contributed to Europe's failure to consider the basic economic conditions for an efficient and durable monetary union.

Not everyone in Europe ignored the OCA criteria. Britain's refusal to join the EMU reflected its recognition of the failure of many member countries to meet the OCA conditions. Britain's chancellor of the exchequer (minister of finance) Gordon Brown said in 1997 that

> the euro was a risk because interest rates appropriate for one part of the area were not necessarily right for another. It was also a risk because all countries were not growing in harmony and because Europe's countries did not appear to have the flexibility to adjust their economies to crises or even the very tough discipline of a single currency.[158]

OCA Not OK?

Since political needs dominated economic needs, key EMU decision makers tended to disregard OCA-related considerations.[159] In
1997, Jean-Claude Trichet, at that time governor of the Banque
de France and later Duisenberg's successor as ECB president, remarked, "everything is done to construct the euro area as an optimum currency area"—an exceptional statement at the time.[160]

Germany's chancellor, Helmut Kohl, and France's president,
François Mitterrand, echoed the prevalent attitude toward OCA-
related issues. David Marsh notes that these two leaders "shared a
taste for the lessons of history and *a disregard for economics*" (italics mine).[161] Politicians who took this stance were supported by a
substantial amount of research published during the 1990s that
questioned the relevance of OCA theory.

In 1987, Peter Robson pointed out that OCA lacked a coherent and quantifiable framework for comparing the conditions for
successful monetary union.[162] The list of conditions provides no in-
dication of which conditions are most important and which are minor. George Tavlas labeled this "the problem of inconclusiveness."[163]
What would be the conclusion if, say, five of the eight conditions
are satisfied sufficiently and three are not satisfied, or are satisfied
only in a very limited way? Do some of the conditions need to be
fulfilled stringently (need to have), whereas others are more flexible
(nice to have)? What about trade-offs? For example, if the factor
of production labor is immobile throughout the monetary union,
wouldn't highly mobile capital, that other major factor of production, offset that to some degree? The OCA approach, it was noted,
could produce significant inconsistencies.[164]For example, very open
economies are usually small economies that are also less diversified.
So the criteria for openness and diversity may not be compatible.

In 1992 the authors of the report *One Market, One Money*—
the bible for EMU supporters—argued that no existing theory was

sufficient to assess the costs and benefits of monetary union.[165] The OCA theory's shortcomings, the report noted, were likely to underestimate the benefits to member countries. The argument was essentially a justification for going ahead with the EMU despite the failure to meet several of the OCA criteria.

The new classical school, led by Nobel Prize winner Robert Lucas of the University of Chicago, struck another blow to the relevance of OCA theory. Their findings called into question the government's ability to intelligently apply monetary and fiscal policy.[166] The implication was that the loss of independent monetary policy and an adjustable exchange rate for a country joining a monetary union was close to irrelevant, as these tools were likely to be used inappropriately, with demonstrably negative results.[167]

Endogenous Manna

As far as the EMU was concerned, the final nail in the OCA theory's coffin was the finding by economists Jeffrey Frankel and Andrew Rose that countries that do not satisfy the OCA conditions as they enter the union may begin to satisfy the conditions after they've joined.[168] Economists referred to this phenomenon as the *endogeneity* of OCA. In plain language, it means that the euro area could turn into an optimum currency area *after* its effective launching— just get the thing up and running and a well-functioning monetary union will just come about.

Some economists, including Peter Kenen and Barry Eichengreen, observed that monetary union tightens trade ties between member countries.[169] This observation led Jeffrey Frankel and Andrew Rose to predict that

> continued European trade liberalization can be expected to result in more tightly correlated European business cycles, making a common European currency both more likely and more desirable. Indeed, monetary union

itself may lead to a further boost to trade integration
and hence business cycle symmetry. Countries which
join EMU, no matter what their motivation, may satisfy OCA criteria *ex post* even if they do not *ex ante*![170]

This argument was hotly contested. Some economists concluded on the basis of the American experience that increased integration leads to increased specialization, worsening the problem
of asymmetric shocks and reducing the desirability of monetary
union.[171]

After Frankel and Rose's analysis, researchers investigated several other routes that might strengthen the endogeneity of OCA
conditions. Looking into financial integration, economic integration as manifested through price and trade movements, symmetry of economic shocks, and product and labor markets, Paul
De Grauwe and Francesco Mongelli concluded that "the different
endogeneities…towards optimal currency areas are at work. How
strong these endogeneities are and how quickly they do their work
remains to be seen."[172]

On top of the other critiques of OCA theory, the endogeneity argument seemed like a gift from heaven for EMU supporters.
Simply put, the endogeneity argument allowed politicians to claim
that the conditions for a well-running monetary union would automatically be met once the whole project got started. Why bother
about them ahead of time?

It's no accident, then, that the Maastricht Treaty did not elaborate on the OCA conditions. Instead, the political decision makers
came up with convergence criteria.[173] Since trade unions and left-
wing political parties would have objected to explicit mention of
the necessity of, for example, more labor mobility, these OCA conditions were excluded from the convergence criteria. Fiscal federalism and political union were far out of reach in the run-up to the
monetary union, so including them in entrance criteria would have

made the whole operation simply impossible *a fortiori*. Instead, decision makers chose criteria on inflation, interest rates, budget deficits, and government debt.

Over time, the deficit and debt criteria would prevent government debt from reaching destabilizing levels and would keep the ECB from needing to monetize government debt. In addition, the lack of fiscal redistribution mechanisms in the case of an asymmetric shock would matter less in a system characterized by strong respect for the deficit and debt criteria. Strict adherence to these criteria in financially healthy EMU member countries would almost certainly improve public finances. The convergence criteria for inflation reflect the OCA condition regarding similar inflation rates, and the convergence of long-term interest rates is parallel to the OCA conditions of financial integration and the openness of economies.

Stalled Progress

The Maastricht Treaty's convergence criteria only partially reflect the traditional OCA conditions. The criteria focus primarily on cyclical movements in financial indicators, such as budget deficits and government debt. Convergence in the real economies of the member states of the monetary union, so crucial to the OCA conditions, was largely absent from the Maastricht Treaty criteria.

Four of the OCA conditions were largely or totally unfulfilled at the start of the EMU. These conditions can be divided into two categories—the first including political integration and fiscal integration, and the second made up of labor mobility and price and wage flexibility. When the euro crisis began in the fall of 2009, these unfulfilled conditions suddenly came to the forefront.

Angel Ubide, director of global economics at Tudor Investment Corporation, argued in the spring of 2010 that "European leaders must now make a clear-cut decision: Either they move on and complete the Economic and Monetary Union that is needed to underpin the euro, or they accept the risk that the eurozone will fail in its current form."[174] In other words, to avoid failure of the eurozone, leaders must fulfill the four outstanding OCA criteria.

Regarding the first group of unfulfilled conditions, little real progress has been made toward political or fiscal union. Early evidence of deeper fiscal convergence among the EMU member states soon proved illusory.[175] Several observers, among them the late eminent economist and member of the first ECB executive board Tommaso Padoa-Schioppa,[176] claimed that the policy infrastructure at the start of the twenty-first century amounted to a partial political union.

The Stability and Growth Pact (SGP), which had provided some rules in the absence of a sufficient political and fiscal union, failed miserably. The initial purpose of the SGP was to install permanent fiscal discipline. In line with the Maastricht Treaty, it stipulated that EMU member countries needed to keep annual budget deficits below 3 percent of GDP and government debt below or approaching 60 percent of GDP. Countries that broke these rules were required to provide a remedial plan to the European Commission. Those that broke the rules three years in a row were subject to fines as high as 0.5 percent of GDP.

In terms of moral hazard, restrictions on how member countries could manage their public finances and penalties for breaking the rules were crucial. Applied to the EMU, the concept of moral hazard deals with the fact that the governments of member countries might (and likely would) behave differently knowing that membership in the EMU was essentially a safety net. Regardless of pacts and formal agreements to the contrary, a member country facing serious financial problems would likely receive help from the other members. On top of that, the ECB potentially provides additional insurance. While the ECB statutes explicitly forbade creating money to finance public debts, the bank might be compelled to provide direct or indirect bailouts to member countries with unmanageable debt.[177]

The SGP "proved to be nothing more than a paper tiger."[178] It failed completely for two reasons: it had no teeth, and it defined debt too narrowly. In the words of Charles Wyplosz, one of Europe's leading economists,

> The Pact never worked and cannot work because it presupposes that a sovereign government can be told what to do with its budget…. Fiscal discipline is and remains a deep-seated national prerogative of each national government and parliament. The inescapable implication is that the Stability Pact must be decentralised to where authority lies.[179]

According to German economists Michael Burda and Stefan Gerlach, the SGP

> failed because nothing happened when governments broke the rules…. The Pact blithely assumed that governments were in control of their revenue and spending at all times, and that they would set aside short-term political considerations in the interest of long-run fiscal stability. Violations, it was hoped, would be obvious to all and swiftly punished.[180]

In October 2002, the president of the European Commission, the Italian Romano Prodi, referred to the SGP as being "stupid." From the very beginning, discussions on the SGP's remedial plans and limitations were a joke. The issue was not the substance of the plans but how to sell them to the market and to the public. In 2003, Germany and France flagrantly breached the SGP budget limits—essentially killing the pact.

Given German policymakers' strong insistence on stringent budget limits and debt ceilings (largely meant to convince the German public that the euro could not be derailed by the irresponsible fiscal policies of southern member states), it's ironic that Germany failed to meet the SGP criteria. In 2005, an attempt was made to revise the SGP with more flexible rules. Despite a heavy investment of political capital and energy, this attempt failed miserably. Astonishingly, as late as 2010, some commentators still argued that the SGP was just the fiscal union the EMU needed.[181]

Germany Showing the Way

Concern about the second group of convergence criteria—labor mobility and price and wage flexibility—translated to an intense focus on labor, product, and financial markets. The Organisation for Economic Co-operation and Development (OECD) observed several close links between these markets. For example, countries with stringent product market regulations tend toward restrictive employment protection legislation.[182] These issues offered a unique opportunity to test the endogeneity theory of OCA criteria: Did the creation of the monetary union lead to greater labor mobility and increased price and wage flexibility?

Research on market functioning within the eurozone has not yet provided a clear answer, although the negative argument seemed to carry more weight. One widely quoted research paper concluded that structural changes to markets that increased their flexibility slowed after the EMU's creation—a flat contradiction of the endogeneity theory.[183] Later research uncovered "significant correlations between the speed of adoption of structural reforms in the goods market and the adoption of the euro" but no evidence "that the adoption of the euro has accelerated labor market reforms in the primary [labor] market."[184]

In such sectors as energy and telecommunications, competition certainly increased, to the benefit of the consumer. But overall, efforts to create the mechanisms for timely and smooth economic adjustments were insufficient, especially in terms of instituting labor markets. As one study concluded in 2010,

> Despite the fact that there has been significant progress in the legal and political framework of the free movement of workers, as well as favourable opinion on free movement among the EU citizens, labor mobility is still very low...a number of legal, administrative, cultural and behavioural barriers[remain].[185]

Efforts to make the necessary structural adjustments to labor and product markets varied among the EMU member countries. Especially in the southern region, many countries failed to improve their market systems. Countries like Greece and Portugal seemed unaware of how the entry of Eastern European countries into the EMU would affect their own competitive positions.[186] Labor costs were low in Poland, Hungary, Slovakia, and the Czech Republic, and these countries had at least as much human capital as southern Europe. As a result, Eastern Europe's competitiveness soon eclipsed that of Greece and Portugal.

Unlike most other eurozone members, Germany did pursue structural changes to its economy, especially its labor markets. Following reunification, Germany's economic performance was dismal. The country's growth lagged behind that of most other EMU members. Unemployment increased from 7.5 percent in 1992 to 11.5 percent in 1997. After a slight drop to 9.5 percent in 2001, it shot up again to a new high of almost 12 percent by 2005. Germany's problems at the start of the twenty-first century were to a considerable extent the result of entering the monetary union with an exchange rate that was too high.

It took a government coalition of socialists and Green Party members to revolutionize German economic policy. In 2003, socialist chancellor Gerhard Schröder launched his Agenda 2010, which aimed to reverse the social and economic decline that by then had plagued Germany for more than a decade. The nucleus of the agenda was the recommendations of the Committee for Modern Services in the Labor Market, better known as the Hartz Committee (after its chairman, Peter Hartz, the human resources manager of the Volkswagen Group).[187]

The Hartz recommendations were implemented in stages, the fourth of which (Hartz IV) included the most sweeping changes. Public employment services were reorganized and training programs redesigned. New mechanisms were installed for wage subsidization and stimulation of business start-ups. Hartz IV limited unemployment benefits over time and substantially cut benefits for those who refused job offers or training programs. It significantly raised the firm size limit for layoff restrictions. Under strong pressure from their members, who were very anxious to keep their threatened jobs, labor unions agreed to a prolonged period of moderation in wage demands.

Although economists disagree on how large a role the Hartz IV measures played in Germany's economic turnaround, most would give them significant credit.[188] By 2006, Germany's economic growth was higher than the eurozone average. After the worst recession since World War II, Germany was experiencing stronger economic activity than any other eurozone country. Its unemployment rate, which had declined to 7.2 percent by 2008, was the most spectacular indicator of the German revival. The employment rate, or the percentage of the working-age population effectively employed, had risen from 69 percent in 2000 to 74 percent in 2008. Drastic and often painful structural adjustments had turned Germany into the most competitive economy in the eurozone.

"A Currency without a Country"

The benefits of a monetary union are very real, but so are the associated costs. These costs tend to increase with the degree of divergence between the union's real characteristics and the OCA criteria. It would be quite an understatement to say that in the years before the start of the monetary union, the advantages were overrated and the disadvantages were brushed under the carpet.

The euro project's major disadvantages relate to what some have called the "unprecedented institutional structure" of the EMU. This structure combines a single monetary policy, managed by the ECB, with multiple economic, budgetary, and regulatory policies, managed by the independent governments of the member countries.[189] Some analysts consider this mismatch a "fundamental problem for the euro" and conclude that "the euro is a currency without a country."[190]

The eurozone's lack of coordination with respect to the banking industry and the financial markets became obvious during the financial crisis. It was also a major obstacle to recovery from that crisis. Paul De Grauwe, professor of economics at Belgium's University of Leuven, wrote in 2003 that "in an integrated eurowide banking system, the present structure of supervision and regulatory control will make it difficult to prevent and to manage financial crises. One can only hope that the necessary institutional changes will occur before the next financial crisis."[191]

The Lisbon Agenda, adopted by the European Council in March 2000, formed a blueprint for the alignment of economic policies with a focus on competitive markets. Labor markets were to take center stage. Unconsciously, the creators of the Lisbon Agenda had essentially borrowed the findings of OCA theory. The purpose of the agenda was to transform Europe into the world's most dynamic and competitive economy by 2010.[192] Doing so would bring about greater convergence in the economic performance of the member states. Addressing the issues of low productivity and stagnant economic growth was the first step.

By the Lisbon Agenda's tenth anniversary, its near-total failure was widely recognized. A comprehensive analysis of the agenda's results led Simon Tilford and Philip Whyte of the Centre for European Reform to conclude that

> few member states have come close to hitting the targets they set themselves in 2000, and the gap between the best and the worst performing countries is arguably wider in 2010 than it was in 2000.... It is hard to shake off the nagging suspicion that most EU member states' reform paths would not have been very different if Lisbon had never existed [since] there has been no more policy convergence within the EU than there has been between the EU and the rest of the OECD.[193]

From its inception, the EMU suffered from many shortcomings and structural flaws. Political considerations forced economic concerns to take a back seat. Given the diverse economic structures of the member countries and differences in their productivity levels and dominant policy views, the founding fathers of EMU took a major risk. In the early years of monetary union, it seemed like a risk well worth taking; a decade into the twenty-first century, it seemed a lot less worthwhile.

Chapter 3

From hero to (almost) zero

I N JANUARY 2008, GERMANY'S MINISTER OF FINANCE, Peer Steinbrück, declared, "My feeling about the euro's success is close to euphoric. It is one of the greatest success stories in the history of the European Community."[194] Steinbrück was far from alone in his view on the first decade of the euro and monetary union in Europe. In May 2008, the European Commission described the European monetary union as

> a resounding success.... Within the space of a decade, (the euro) has clearly become the second most important currency in the world; it has brought economic stability; it has promoted economic and financial integration, and generated trade and growth among its members; and its framework for sound and sustainable public finances helps ensure that future generations can continue to benefit from the social systems that Europe is justly famous for.[195]

Otmar Issing, the member of the ECB's executive board from 1998 to 2006 who is generally considered to be the major architect of the ECB's initial strategy and procedures, said in June 2008, "Today, it is hard to find anybody who denies that the euro has become an astounding success."[196] A few months later, Joaquin Almunia, the member of the European Commission responsible for economic and monetary affairs, repeated the same message:

> The euro…has accumulated a reputation of solidity and stability, and brought overwhelming benefits to the European economy: both to citizens and business…. The Cassandras and sceptics who thought the euro was an impossible project or predicted disaster were proven wrong…. The economic advantages of EMU are overwhelming for all its members.[197]

Almost simultaneously, ECB president Jean-Claude Trichet said in a speech that "the euro is a historic achievement. Its first ten years have been a success…. Europe can be very proud of what it achieved."[198] Certainly Peter Mandelson, business secretary in Gordon Brown's Labour government, agreed with this evaluation. In June 2009, Mandelson caused a small uproar in the United Kingdom by describing the euro as "a great success" and by strongly favouring Britain's accession to the monetary union.[199]

Praise for EMU and the euro did not only come from government officials. Many private sector economists were also enthusiastic. For example, Erik Nielsen, European chief economist at Goldman Sachs, wrote in June 2008 that "so far the ECB, the Euro and the Euro-zone economy have all the hallmarks of a success, including… contributing to an unprecedented degree of financial stability."[200] When the EMU project and its crown jewel, the euro, celebrated their tenth anniversary on January 1, 2009, many European politicians, economists, and commentators were on the same page.

Untimely Celebrations

At first, optimism among European policymakers, private analysts, and economists seemed warranted. The introduction of the euro had gone smoothly, and at the height of the financial crisis, the monetary union protected the smaller member states with oversized banking sectors, such as Belgium and Ireland. Nonmember states, such as Iceland and Hungary, experienced banking and currency crises that led to deep recessions and huge increases in unemployment and budget deficits.

The ECB's performance was a major component of the EMU's perceived success. The ECB seemed to have inherited the credibility of its role model, the Bundesbank. The executive board and the governing council steered monetary policy with confidence. Despite consistently hitting, and occasionally even overshooting, its inflation target of "below, but close to 2 percent," the ECB dealt with various crises in a way that earned it almost universal praise. Shocks to the system during that decade included the dot-com bubble's explosion, the September 11, 2001 terrorist attacks, wars in Iraq and Afghanistan, a steep rise in oil prices in 2008, and, of course, the financial crisis that began in the summer of 2007.

The ECB's good performance was matched by good economic performance in general for the euro area. Comparison with U.S. performance during the first decade of the euro's existence puts this achievement into context. The euro area did not outperform the United States, but it didn't lag behind, either (see **Table 3.1**). Real economic growth during the first decade of the euro's existence was, on average, 2.1 percent in the eurozone, compared with 2.6 percent in the United States. The growth rate of GDP per head of the population was equal in the eurozone and the United States. Employment grew faster in the eurozone, but the average unemployment rate stayed well above the U.S. rate. Inflation in the eurozone was, on average, below the American rates. Government debt was nearly equal, but the eurozone performed slightly better on average in terms of government deficit. The eurozone showed a small external surplus (0.4 percent of GDP) whereas the United States had been deep into deficit territory for years (–4.7 percent of GDP in 2008).

Table 3.1 The euro's first decade

Comparison with the U.S., 1999 - 2008

	Euro Area	USA
REAL GDP GROWTH		
• per year	2.1	2.6
• per head of population	1.6	1.6
EMPLOYMENT		
• average growth rate p.a.	1.3	1.0
UNEMPLOYMENT		
• average rate	8.3	5.0
INFLATION		
• average rate	2.2	2.9
GOVERNMENT BUDGET		
• in % GDP	-1.8	-2.4
GOVERNEMENT DEBT		
• in % GDP, end of period	67.2	67.5
EXTERNAL POSITION		
• in % GDP	0.4	-4.7

Source: Buti etal., 2010

Dark Clouds Gathering

Beneath the euro area's overall satisfactory performance, however, disequilibria lurked. There were five primary imbalances:

1. Large current account deficits (implying dependence on import of foreign capital into the deficit countries)
2. Major asset bubbles accompanied by excessive credit creation (and hence increased risks to bank solvency)
3. Huge government deficits
4. Mounting debt
5. Loss of international competitiveness for several member countries

Each of these disequilibria was linked to the others. For example, excessive credit creation fueled inflation, which in turn contributed to wage increases that hurt international competitiveness. Combined with mounting government deficits, these developments jacked up current account deficits.

In hindsight, it seems unbelievable that the danger signs went unnoticed. However, political decision makers persisted in their blind optimism. Criticism of the monetary union was not taken lightly. Although warning flags were raised in closed meetings at the ECB, the European Commission, the OECD, the IMF, and major think tanks, they rarely made it out into the open, and they were brought up even less often in final political decision making. At best, critical remarks were politely ignored.

Some economists saw the dark clouds gathering and refused to keep silent. At the height of the fanfare surrounding the tenth anniversary of the euro's launch, the London-based Centre for European Reform published an essay by Simon Tilford, its chief economist, that began, "the euro is riding high on the foreign exchange markets, and the financial crisis has graphically illustrated that euro membership provides a safe haven. On the face of it, this seems to be a strange time to question the stability of the currency union." But, Tilford wrote, "the economic crisis threatens to exacerbate underlying imbalances within the eurozone, thereby creating difficulties for some of its members," further pointing to increasing concerns of investors that "some member-states will suffer economic stagnation, and that this will raise doubts over their solvency, and conceivably even over their continued membership of the euro."[201]

Three years earlier, Tilford had fired a warning salvo in a paper entitled "Will the Eurozone Crack?" At a moment when most were heaping the project with praise, Tilford warned that it was

> far too soon to talk about EMU being a success. The single currency was supposed to bring Europe together, but it risks becoming a source of economic dislocation and political division…. The discipline being required for successful membership has been badly underestimated by most members, bringing into doubt the long-term viability of the single currency…. Further

delays in implementing microeconomic reforms and institutional changes would greatly increase the risk that EMU unravels.[202]

Around the time Tilford voiced his unfashionable warning, another British citizen was speaking prophetic words. Nigel Lawson, a longtime skeptic on European monetary union who served as chancellor of the exchequer under Margaret Thatcher, argued in April 2007,

> EMU is a remarkable achievement. However, the Russians' feat of putting a man into space was also a remarkable achievement. Even if it doesn't all end in tears—and so much political will has been invested in it that the politicians will move heaven and earth to make it a success—whether it will achieve any great benefit is, like the achievement of putting Yuri Gagarin into space, a question that we cannot at the moment answer.[203]

Papandreou's Tipping Point

The disequilibria within the monetary union increased gradually during its first decade. When the recession hit in late 2008, markets suddenly realized that untenable situations had indeed built up. Once the severity of the recession became clear, crisis within the eurozone developed at lightning speed. The markets feared—correctly, as it turned out—that this recession would further aggravate the already existing disequilibria.

Severe financial crises always have tipping points. More often than not, a seemingly inconsequential declaration or event, or even a mere suspicion, takes on overwhelming importance and gets the crisis train going. As far as the great financial crisis of 2007–09 is concerned, the collapse of the American market for subprime mortgage loans triggered the crisis, but it soon became obvious that the financial and banking sectors and the economy at large had bigger problems than the complications emanating from a bunch of worthless, even fraudulent American mortgages.

In the words of British economist Roger Bootle, "Attributing the disaster of 2007/9 to subprime is rather like saying that the first World War was caused by the assassination of Archduke Franz Ferdinand in Sarajevo in 1914. Given the state of the financial system, if the subprime crisis hadn't happened, something else would have."[204]

In the case of the euro crisis, Greece's newly elected prime minister George Papandreou's admission in October 2009 that his country's budget deficit was much larger than anyone had officially admitted up to that point served as the tipping point. To the consternation of the European public and the financial markets, Papandreou declared that Greece's 2009 budget deficit would at least double the 6 percent of GDP put forward by the old Greek government.

At the beginning of 2009, the Greek government had promised a budget deficit of 3.7 percent. It soon became abundantly clear that the Greek government had lied about its budget deficits to get into the EMU. American investment bank Goldman Sachs had, through some creative financial engineering, helped Athens hide its official budget deficit and government debt numbers.[205] The main drivers of Greece's derailing public finances were its bloated public sector; runaway spending on health care, pensions, and other entitlements; widespread corruption; and poor-to-nonexistent tax administration.

Let there be no mistake: If Papandreou hadn't confessed, to paraphrase Roger Bootle, something else would have sparked the sovereign debt crisis in Europe. The situation had become thoroughly untenable, and Greece was just the tip of the iceberg. The discovery of Greece's chicanery drew almost immediate attention to a host of major problems within the euro area, from huge imbalances in the current accounts to the fragility of Europe's banking sector.

Also troubling was the fact that even during years of strong economic growth, several members had failed to significantly improve—in some cases, even maintain—their longer-term fiscal positions.[206] The recession and the fiscal cost of financial and banking rescue operations made these problems more severe and more visible. Analysts and investors began to realize that the problems within the eurozone were not isolated cases of local mismanagement. The real and potential crisis situations were directly related to fundamental faultlines in the monetary union.

Whatever the broader picture, Papandreou's confession in itself created a shock, both in the political world and in the financial markets. Greece's minister of finance, Yiannos Papantoniou, declared in the summer of 1999, "We must enter the euro with a clean sheet on all the criteria,"[207] thus contributing to the illusion of newfound Greek financial orthodoxy. In March 2000, Greece formally requested entrance to the EMU. On the basis of their intensely massaged data, the European leaders approved Greece's entry at a July 2000 summit. This was viewed as a major turning point in the history of a country long seen as untrustworthy when it came to budgetary and financial matters.

Interest Rates on Steroids

EMU membership worked monetary wonders for Greece for two reasons. The first was the ECB's monetary policy. Of course, the ECB's only option was to aim for a hypothetical average economic condition for the eurozone as a whole. Policy was largely determined by the economies of Germany, France, and Italy. This was especially true when there was substantial convergence in economic performance between these three countries. When the Big Three experienced low inflation, weak growth, and high unemployment, the ECB set a low nominal policy interest rate (see **Graph 3.1**). Of course, this rate also applied to member countries with higher inflation and faster economic growth.

Second, euro membership almost immediately brought down market interest rates and risk premiums. Just as the ECB had in-

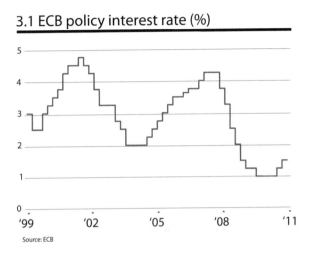

3.1 ECB policy interest rate (%)

Source: ECB

herited the credibility of the Bundesbank, the same was passed on to Greece. The ten-year real interest rate in Greece fell from 5 percent in 1999 to zero in 2005 (see **Graph 3.2**). The country risk premium on Greece virtually vanished.

The markets and the rating agencies went along with the official storyline on Greece's newfound seriousness in economic, budgetary, and financial matters. The spread between Greek and German bonds almost disappeared, meaning that the Greek government could borrow money at a rate just marginally higher than Europe's most creditworthy nation.[208] "Greece," wrote financial commentator Matthew

3.2 Real interest rates in the eurozone (1)

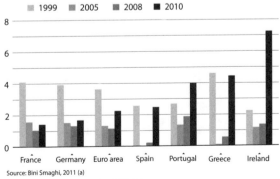

Source: Bini Smaghi, 2011 (a)

(1) Nominal 10 year interest rate minus HICP inflation

Lynn, "was no longer a wacky fringe country, of interest only to brave speculators and emerging market funds. At the end of a long journey, it was now right in the mainstream of European finance. It was a rock-solid, A-rated nation, as creditworthy as Germany."[209]

EMU membership also worked wonders for Ireland, Portugal, and Spain. Real interest rates there fell substantially (see **Graph 3.2**), which made borrowing money much more attractive. Monetary union also brought these countries into what I call a *europhoric* state of mind.

The fall in real interest rates was, of course, the result of a steep fall in nominal interest rates combined with an inflation rate that remained above Germany's and above the average for the euro area (see **Graph 3.3**). The boost to aggregate demand caused by these falling real interest rates led to higher economic growth (see **Graph 3.4**). It's no coincidence that among the Club Med countries (as Greece, Italy, Ireland, Portugal, and Spain were collectively known), Portugal was one of the weakest performers in terms of economic growth, since it also saw the smallest declines in its real interest rates. The superior growth performance of the Club Med countries undoubtedly contributed to markets' and decision makers' lack of attention to the underlying imbalances.

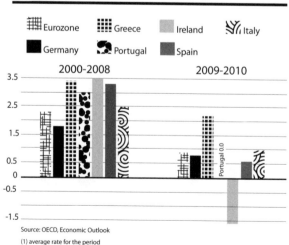

3.3 Inflation in the eurozone (1)

Eurozone Greece Ireland Italy
Germany Portugal Spain

2000-2008   2009-2010

Source: OECD, Economic Outlook
(1) average rate for the period

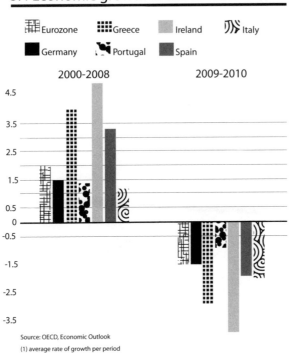

3.4 Economic growth in the eurozone (1)

Legend: Eurozone, Greece, Ireland, Italy, Germany, Portugal, Spain

2000-2008   2009-2010

Source: OECD, Economic Outlook
(1) average rate of growth per period

Higher economic growth gradually pushed up inflation, which in turn reduced the real cost of borrowing even more. In fact, the real cost of borrowing money even turned negative in some cases. With interest rates way too low, given that inflation rate and country risk premiums were no longer a consideration for the markets, internal spending far exceeded internal production. This led to rapidly increasing deficits on the current account of these countries' balance of payments. Financing these deficits was no problem, since foreign banks and other financial institutions saw no currency risk.

The Club Med countries accumulated enormous current account deficits, which were accompanied by huge, and increasing, current account surpluses in countries such as Germany and the Netherlands (see **Graph 3.5**). The balance sheets of financial institutions throughout the euro area were loaded with more and more bonds and other paper produced by the deficit countries.

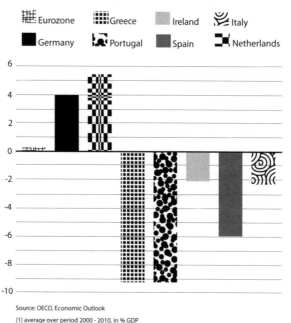

3.5 Current accounts in the eurozone (1)

Source: OECD, Economic Outlook
(1) average over period 2000 - 2010, in % GDP

Becoming Uncompetitive

The very low (and in real, inflation-adjusted terms, even negative) interest rates the Club Med countries received through their EMU membership pushed up economic growth. One way this growth manifested itself was an enormous boom in the real estate sector. House prices escalated and construction activity increased. This was most extreme in Ireland and Spain, but Greece also experienced higher price increases than the eurozone average (see **Graph 3.6**). In some EMU countries, the real estate bubble was even more pronounced than in the United States. In Greece, Ireland, and Spain, the growth in housing construction was, in real terms, more than 60 percent between 2000 and 2007 (see **Graph 3.7**) whereas the average for the euro area as a whole was 12 percent over the same period.

This mother of all real estate bubbles was fueled by an enormous credit expansion (see **Graph 3.8** on p. 90) that was in part financed

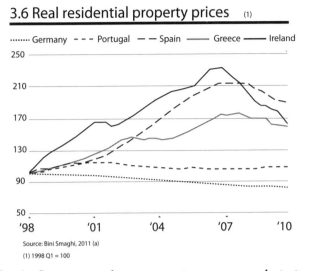

3.6 Real residential property prices (1)

Source: Bini Smaghi, 2011 (a)
(1) 1998 Q1 = 100

by the funds flowing to these countries to cover their increasing current account deficits. Using a type of understatement typical of central bankers' speeches, Lorenzo Bini Smaghi, the Italian member of the ECB executive board, declared early in 2011 that

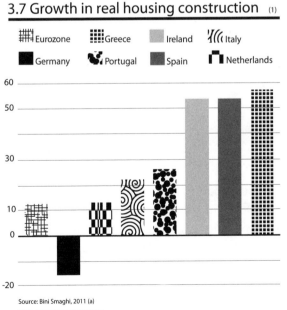

3.7 Growth in real housing construction (1)

Source: Bini Smaghi, 2011 (a)
(1) % change from 2000 to 2007

3.8 Credit expansion in the eurozone (1)

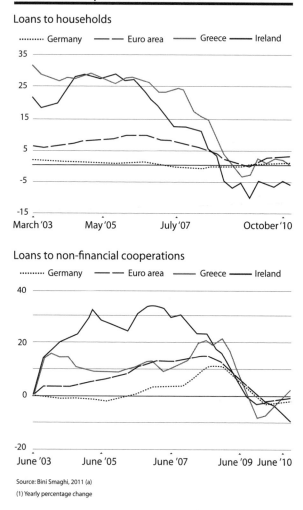

Loans to households

·········· Germany   — — Euro area   ——— Greece ——— Ireland

Loans to non-financial cooperations

·········· Germany   — — Euro area   ——— Greece ——— Ireland

Source: Bini Smaghi, 2011 (a)
(1) Yearly percentage change

no doubt part of the rapid expansion of credit was justi-fied on fundamental grounds. After all, studies by the European Commission during the 1980s and 1990s had promised a sizeable growth dividend from the Single Market and Monetary Union. But, in an environment of large-scale structural change in peripheral economies and their financial systems, distinguishing the impact of

improved fundamentals from that of 'bubble-like' be-
haviour proved a formidable challenge.[210]

The central banks in the Club Med countries that faced a real
estate bubble could have cooled things down by, for example, imposing higher reserve requirements on mortgage loans extended
by the banking sector. The fiscal authorities could have revisited
the fiscal and financial stimuli for real estate activity, and the same
holds for the regulators. But, as *The Economist* argued with respect
to Ireland, "financial regulators were incompetent at best, cronies
at worst"—an argument that holds for all the Club Med countries.[211] The one-size-fits-all monetary policy and the virtual disap-
pearance of country risk premiums created a short-term real estate
bonanza. The Portuguese and Greek governments added more fuel
to the fire. Portugal's budget deficit remained wide, and Greece's
widened even further (see **Graph 3.9** on the next page).

Meanwhile, Ireland and Spain kept their government budgets
under control. Official debt levels as a percent of GDP even declined in the years leading up to 2008 (see **Graph 3.10** on p. 93).[212]
"Before the financial crisis," one observer noted, "Ireland and Spain
were the poster children for responsible fiscal policy."[213] However,
tax receipts in both countries came to depend heavily on real estate
transactions. When the bubble burst, tax receipts evaporated.

The erosion of Club Med countries' international cost competitiveness was a major consequence of the real estate bubble.
Enormous demand pushed up wages in the real estate sector. The
same was true in government-controlled branches of the economy.
Because these countries are highly unionized, these wage increases
spilled over into other sectors of the economy, including those exposed to international competition. Since productivity couldn't
keep pace with the wage increases, international cost competitiveness as measured by relative labor costs went down the drain (see
Graph 3.11 on p. 93). The loss of international competitiveness

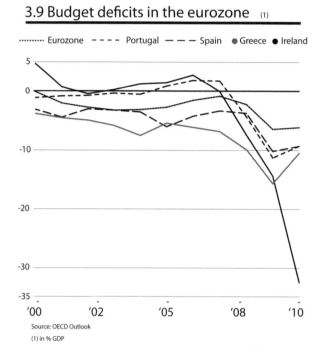

3.9 Budget deficits in the eurozone (1)

········· Eurozone   - - - - Portugal   — — — Spain   ● Greece   ● Ireland

Source: OECD Outlook
(1) in % GDP

was impressive when compared with the eurozone average; compared with Germany, it was astounding.

That *europhoric* state of mind I mentioned earlier deepened the loss of international competitiveness. The euphoria created by the monetary miracles that befell the Club Med countries took away any sense of urgency they may have felt to improve the efficiency and the innovative and entrepreneurial capacities of their economies. Why bother with such unpopular and electorally sensitive issues when the manna of economic growth, more employment, and increased welfare is falling from the euro heavens? Product markets remained highly regulated and/or dominated by entities that thrived on crony capitalism. Under the pressure of powerful labor unions, byzantine regulations, and restrictive closed-shop practices, labor markets remained immobile and inflexible.[214]

3.10 Government debt in the eurozone (1)

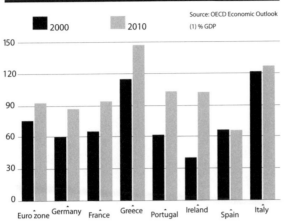

These countries' lack of internal competitiveness was visible in meaningful international rankings. In the World Bank's ranking of 183 countries doing business in 2010, Portugal ranked forty-eighth, Spain was sixty-second, Italy was seventy-eighth, and Greece was 109th. In the 2010 International Institute for Management Development (IMD) World Competitiveness Yearbook, Ireland ranked

3.11 Relative unit labor costs (1)

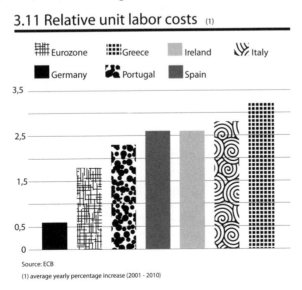

3.12 Spreads on 10-year bonds (1)

● Portugal   ● Spain   ● Ireland   ● Greece

10/01/2009   08/01/2011

Source: Bloomberg
(1) in 00 basispoints as compared with Germany

twenty-first among fifty-eight countries. Spain was thirty-sixth, Portugal thirty-seventh, Italy fortieth, and Greece forty-sixth.

Booming internal demand led to large current account deficits, making these countries dependent on international money. The loss of international competitiveness deepened this dependence. It's astonishing that the situation went on for so long. In the end, European policymakers and citizens found out the hard way about Stein's Law—the rule coined in the 1980s by Herbert Stein, chairman of U.S. President Richard Nixon's council of advisors. Stein claimed that "if something is unsustainable, it will stop." The *euro-phoria* ended in late 2009.

Saving Athens

No advanced European country had faced sovereign default since 1948. By the beginning of 2010, Greece was close to ending that sixty-two-year run. Papandreou's confession was followed almost immediately by rapid increase in the spreads of Greece's bonds as measured against German *bunds* (considered the safest investment in the euro area). (See **Graph 3.12.**) Investors fled Greek paper, and the country found it increasingly difficult to raise the funds to cover its deficits. It quickly became clear that this was more than a liquidity crisis. Financial markets made it unequivocally clear that an EMU member country's solvency was at stake. The sovereign debt crisis within the euro area was there for all to see.

The panic over Greece brought other EMU countries under scrutiny in the context of the revived risk aversion that followed the financial crisis. Portugal, Ireland, and Spain also saw significant increases in their bond spreads. The financial market became increasingly suspicious of these countries' financial and economic stability.

The prospect of a full-blown euro crisis was all too real by early 2010. Political leaders desperately tried to calm the markets, but their attempts seemed to backfire. In February 2010, the European Council issued a declaration stating that the safeguarding of financial stability was considered a "collective responsibility" with clear hints "at the highest political level [that]…the European Council would do 'whatever it takes' to stabilize the euro."[215] In the meantime, German Chancellor Angela Merkel, supported by countries such as the Netherlands, Finland, and Austria, dug in her heels and refused to bail out profligate euro members.

The crisis deepened all the same, as Greece, Portugal, and Spain experienced further credit rating downgrades in March and April. Default by Greece, which would lead to an immediate sovereign debt restructuring, was considered, but the risk to the fragile Western European banks was deemed too great. By early May, the bond spread increases of all the Club Med countries were making their financing costs unbearable. Spreads of Greek bonds over German bonds approached a record-high 1,000 basis points.

It was becoming unlikely that Greece would be able to find the financing it needed just to stay in operation. In hopes of preventing Greece's open bankruptcy, European authorities put together a rescue package of 110 billion euros. Euro members' contributions accounted for 80 billion; the IMF put up the remaining 30 billion.[216] The Maastricht and Lisbon treaties' "no bailout" clauses had gone out the window.

The deal specified that the Greek authorities had to slash spending and increase taxes to reduce the budget deficit and stop the uncontrollable increase in government debt. Furthermore, the Greek government was required to take significant measures to improve its competitiveness, to restructure its economy, and to improve the quality of the economic data it provided. Athens was put under the curatorship of the IMF and the EU and was expected to provide interim reports on its progress every three months. The rescue package would allow Greece to finance itself without a return to the market until 2012, assuming the Greek government adhered to all the stipulations.

Almost immediately, the markets expressed serious doubt about that prospect. Greece was in a Catch-22. One camp in the markets just couldn't believe that Greece would deliver on its promises and thought default was inevitable. The other was prepared to believe that the Greek government would try its best. Nonetheless, this strategy was doomed from the beginning. Massive spending cuts combined with unavoidable tax increases would deepen the recession, further increase unemployment, erode government receipts, jack up expenditures, and widen the budget deficit even more. By courageously following the austerity program, Greece would lose its last ounce of creditworthiness.

The traditional way out of such a vicious cycle is currency devaluation, which boosts external demand and stimulates internal production. Of course, devaluation is not an option in a monetary union.[217] With international competitiveness way out of line, a devaluation-like effect can be achieved through a massive internal deflation with *nominal* wage cuts. Whether Greece could survive such a hellish combination of deficit cutting and internal deflation was very much in doubt.

A Three-Tiered Scheme

Even with the 110-billion-euro rescue package on the table, finan-cial markets kept their distance from Greece. Moreover, the danger that Portugal, Ireland, and Spain would follow in Greece's foot-steps mounted. The sovereign debt crisis continued as if the Greek package didn't exist. Even worse, the markets loudly proclaimed their belief that sovereign debt default by a euro area member was a very real possibility. They expected European political authorities to find a comprehensive solution to the crisis. Shortly after agree-ment was reached on the Greek rescue package, it became obvious that additional measures were needed if the European authorities wanted to regain control of the situation.

Policymakers referred to the market pressure as speculative folly or irrational market behavior. While this was true to some extent, the way the authorities handled the crises was also much to blame. The main partners publicly disagreed on both the diagnosis of and cures for the crisis. The uncertainty resulting from policymakers' failures to contain and resolve the crisis inspired investment portfolio changes that could be labeled speculative but would more appropriately be defined as responsible management in risk-adjusted terms.

Under extreme pressure from financial markets, the finance min-isters of the twenty-seven EU member states, together with repre-sentatives of the ECB, the European Commission, and the IMF, in May 2010 came up with a massive three-tiered rescue scheme. They launched a 750-billion-euro rescue fund and fundamentally rede-fined the role of the ECB. However, the ECB's top brass accepted their new role only reluctantly, which didn't help the credibility of the rescue scheme.

The first of the three tiers was the creation of the two-part Euro-pean Stabilisation Mechanism (ESM). The European Financial Sta-bility Facility [EFSF], set up to raise 440 billion euros on the basis of guarantees provided by the eurozone countries, was the more important of its two parts. The second part was the creation of a 60-billion-euro supranational facility, the European Financial Stability Mechanism [EFSM], administered by the European Commission.

The second tier of the rescue scheme was 250 billion euros provided by the IMF to supplement the ESM, and the third tier was the ECB's commitment to intervene to prevent major market disruptions and unwarranted defaults. Mistrust among and different priorities of the main negotiating partners led to the vague and complicated nature of the rescue mechanism.[218]

The preparation needed to get the EFSF up and running meant that it would not begin operation until the beginning of August. When the markets reopened the Monday after the rescue scheme was agreed upon, only the ECB could provide the liquidity to stop the crisis from spreading. The ECB acted by creating the Securities Market Programme (SMP), under which it could buy any private and public securities in the secondary market. During the first six months of the SMP, the ECB intervened for close to 70 billion euros. Most of the interventions took place in May and June.

This type of intervention was a departure from the dominant view within the ECB of what central bank independence really meant. ECB president Jean-Claude Trichet and other members of the governing council insisted that the interventions would not lead to new money creation. ECB spokespeople emphasized that the interventions had been inspired by the financial stability mandate and not by concerns about sovereign liquidity or solvency. But the arguments lacked credibility.[219] By trying to disguise the true nature of the interventions, the ECB badly damaged its reputation.

Life in Drama

The meeting at which the rescue scheme was decided was scheduled for May 7 through 9, but actually ran until 2 a.m. on Monday, May 10. The political decision makers were under enormous pressure to come to an agreement before the Asian financial markets opened. Discussions were bitter, especially regarding the new role of the ECB.[220] Most of the issues on the negotiation table divided northern and southern Europe. It is not an oversimplification to talk of a German camp, in which the Netherlands, Austria, and Finland reside, and a French camp harboring most of the other member states. Many of the discussions were a continuation of the historical opposition between the Germans and the French.

Germany and its partners wanted to restore budget discipline, international competitiveness, and financial stability to the peripheral Club Med countries as quickly and decisively as possible, with no loss of independence to the ECB. The French camp wanted more solidarity from the northern countries and more political control over the ECB.

The discussion finally culminated in an outright fight. At one point, French president Nicolas Sarkozy became so angered by the Germans' stubborn attitude that he threatened to pull France out of the EMU.[221] *The Economist* noted that "Mrs. Merkel's government thinks it is outrageous that it is taxed with euro-scepticism for insisting on tough conditions before bailing out members of the euro who caused their own problems." The Germans felt strongly that the southern argument was intended to make Germany pay for the crisis.[222]

Thomas de Mazière, a confidante of Merkel's, was her chief of staff from 2005 until 2009. Later, he became minister of the interior and in 2011, minister of defense. De Mazière summarized the German position a few days after the meetings:

> Germany wants to provide its loan guarantees on the basis of its own creditworthiness, and not to take on some unlimited liability. All Germans have worked hard to achieve better financing conditions. If we provide loan guarantees for a country that is in trouble, we want to provide those guarantees on the same conditions that we

encounter, as Germany, on the markets. We don't want to turn the EU into a transfer union. France is not as strict as us. The French said it would send a strong signal to the market and facilitate French financing possibilities if we used an average European financing rate. That was not our position and that is why the negotiations went on so late in the night.[223]

The drama continued after the deal was struck. As soon as the news of the creation of the EFSF came out, discussion began on the true nature of this vehicle. As already indicated, each eurozone member was to contribute to the EFSF capital according to its share in the capital of the ECB.

In order to get an AAA rating for the EFSF, each member state had to guarantee 120 percent of its initial allocation. This would make up for the fact that countries that needed to access the facility would not be in a position to contribute in the first place. The rating agencies indicated that for the EFSF to get a AAA rating, the total amount it loaned out could not exceed the contributions of the member states individually rated as AAA—namely, Germany, France, the Netherlands, Austria, and Luxembourg. This left the EFSF with 255 billion euros of financial ammunition instead of the original 440 billion. A further complication was that since the EFSF was created under article 122 of the EU Treaty, it was essentially temporary. The EFSF's life could not continue beyond June 30, 2013.

Weber's Infighting

Drama also continued to surround the SMP, which political leaders had forced on the ECB. In a flagrant breach of central bank etiquette, Bundesbank president and ECB governing council member Axel Weber openly criticized the ECB for going along with the politicians' scheme.[224] "The purchase of government bonds poses significant stability risks and that's why I'm critical toward this part of the ECB council's decision, even in this extraordinary situation," Weber declared immediately after the historic European summit.[225]

Weber's dissent was typical of the German attitude toward the way the crisis was handled. The German press had almost nothing positive to say about the European authorities' financial rescue operations. The *Frankfurter Allgemeine Zeitung*, known for its seriousness and balanced views, argued, "Since a transfer union has been effectively introduced and the central bank is now under political command, the fate of the euro as a soft currency and the failure of the monetary union are certain."[226] Germans in general felt that the costs of the German unification had been severe, and now they were obliged to pay for the reckless behavior of the southern European countries.

The reemergence of the Gang of Four, the renegade professors who had tried to stop the creation of the EMU with a complaint at Germany's Federal Institutional court in early 1998, was a symbol of the German resistance to the management of the crisis.[227] That complaint was rejected, but on the occasion of the Greek bailout constitution they argued that the violation of the Maastricht Treaty's "no bailout" clause rendered the whole euro project unconstitutional, according to German law.[228] Several public opinion polls suggested broad support for this view, with about half of Germans expressing their desire to have their good old D-mark back.[229]

Axel Weber became a symbol for German opposition to the handling of the euro crisis. A few months after the launch of the SMP, Weber declared at a symposium in New York,

> There is no evidence that asset purchases have had any significant impact on average euro-area sovereign bond yields on which euro-area monetary policy must exclusively focus as its main transmission channel. But the SMP risks blurring the different responsibilities between fiscal and monetary policy. As the risks associated with the SMP outweigh its benefits, these securities purchases should now be phased out permanently as part of our non-standard policy measures.[230]

A few weeks later, ECB president Trichet emphasized at a press conference that "the Securities Market Programme is ongoing, I repeat...ongoing" and that an "overwhelming majority" within the ECB was in favour of continuing the bond-buying program in its present form.[231] It did not go unnoticed that Trichet did not use his favorite word regarding the decisions of the ECB: *unanimity.*

Weber, who had exchanged sharp words with Trichet in the ECB's council in September, split from the consensus at the ECB at the end of October. He sided with Merkel, who had claimed that in future debt crises, private bond investors should share the costs of rescuing financially troubled governments rather than leaving taxpayers to foot the bill. These remarks sent considerable shock waves through the markets and made Weber an increasingly controversial figure. Sarkozy let it be known that he found it unacceptable that someone like Weber would become president of the ECB (as was expected to occur when Trichet's term ended in October 2011).

Despite the writing on the wall, Axel Weber surprised most with his February 2011 announcement that he would not seek a second term as president of the Bundesbank—a move that also terminated his candidacy for the top job at the ECB. Disappointed in the way Merkel's government managed the crisis in the eurozone and feeling more and more isolated in the ECB's governing council, the principled Weber clearly saw no other option.

Weber's decision was a major setback for Merkel, as it hampered her attempts to explain European authorities' management of the crisis to a very skeptical German public. Weber returned to his academic career, this time as a professor at the University of Chicago. In mid-February 2011, the German government decided that Axel Weber would be succeeded at the helm of the Bundesbank by Jens Wiedman, Merkel's trusted economic advisor of forty-two years.

Cajas in a Tailspin

Despite its tumultuous birth, the three-tiered scheme was somewhat calming to the markets. For example, the spread of Greek bonds over German ten-year *bunds* came down from 1,000 basis points to less than 500. The spread on Irish bonds went from 300 to less than 200. Interventions by the ECB under its SMP were the main drivers of the improvements in market sentiment. However, before the end of May, market nervousness shot up once more. Market doubts about Greece, Ireland, and Portugal were no longer surprising, but when the markets turned negative on Spain, whose economy is much larger than the economies of the three smaller countries combined, the crisis became an entirely different matter. As Paul Krugman colorfully described it, "The others are tapas, Spain is the main course."[232]

On May 24, the Bank of Spain took control of the savings bank Cajasur after attempts to merge Cajasur with Unicaja, another savings bank, failed. Headquartered in the southern city of Cordoba and one of the largest of the country's forty-five local savings banks (*cajas*), Cajasur had 18 billion euros in assets and five hundred offices, mainly in southern Spain. Imprudent lending during the growth of the real estate bubble had brought the rate of nonperforming loans on Cajasur's books close to 10 percent.

Through its Fund for Orderly Bank Restructuring (FOBR), the Bank of Spain immediately injected 550 million euros into the ailing Cajasur. On the day of Cajasur's seizure by the Bank of Spain, four other savings banks announced their intention to merge. The resulting entity, with 135 billion euros in assets, became Spain's fifth-largest bank.

On that same day, the IMF issued a warning on the Spanish economy's dire situation. The IMF pointed to a dysfunctional labor market, huge overall indebtedness (private as well as public), anemic productivity growth, and weak international competitiveness, arguing that the restructuring of the Spanish banking sector needed to be sped up and that the Bank of Spain should be prepared to intervene promptly if and when needed.

Savings banks control close to half the banking business in Spain, and most are organized in a very archaic way and controlled by local political bosses. Attempts to clean up their balance sheets are highly complicated and politically exhausting affairs. Such a cleanup was sorely needed after many *cajas* got burned financing Spain's real estate bubble. The seizure of Cajasur, combined with the IMF's warning and further downgrades of several other *cajas* by the rating agencies, confirmed the markets' fears about the Spanish banking sector. The markets doubted Spain's ability to keep its public finances sufficiently under control while introducing the necessary structural policies to improve the bleak employment and growth perspectives.

The Cajasur event sent shivers down the spines of European authorities. Fears regarding government solvency fed concern about the health of the banking sector, and vice versa. Data that showed the large French and German banks to have substantial exposure to private and public debt in countries such as Greece, Ireland, Portugal, and Spain did not help the situation.[233] Markets wanted more information on the cross-border links between European banks. Additional pressure came from the ECB's regular hints that the governments needed to act on financial institutions with obvious solvency problems because the ECB couldn't keep them alive forever.

Bogus Tests Fuel Stress

To stop the panic from spreading further, stress tests of the European banks were performed as quickly as possible. Some stress tests already had been performed in September 2009, but the results were not made public, so their impact was minor. This time, markets reacted positively because they immediately linked this initiative to the stress tests performed on nineteen top American banks in the spring of 2009. The American stress tests concluded that ten out of these nineteen banks had inadequate capital—to the global tune of $75 billion. The banks were ordered to raise that capital, and most promptly delivered. Despite the fact that they were initially criticized for being too lenient, the American stress tests were soon recognized as a major turning point in the American banking crisis, largely because the published results contained a wealth of information on the tested financial institutions.

The European stress tests, coordinated by the London-based and thinly staffed Committee of European Banking Supervisors (CEBS)[234] but run by the national authorities, covered ninety-one banks in twenty European countries. Specialists from the ECB were closely involved in the whole process. To pass the tests, the banks' Tier 1 capital needed to stay at 6 percent of total assets or higher. Despite the fact that European banks had raised at least 200 billion euros in fresh capital since the beginning of 2009, the markets estimated that at least twenty of the ninety-one institutions tested needed to further raise their capital by somewhere between 30 and 90 billion euros.[235]

The stress tests were conducted in a disorderly and confrontational way, with the CEBS continuously fighting national regulators on numerous issues. German banks and regulators in particular were reluctant to make the stress tests into a useful exercise. Eurozone members publicly disagreed on whether to publish the test results. Spain announced it would publish the results, in an obvious attempt to diminish the pressure the country was experiencing. Several other countries, including Germany, were less interested in public disclosure. In an attempt to boost investor confidence, and under pressure from the IMF, European leaders finally decided to publish the stress test results.

The results were released toward the end of July. Seven banks were found to be in need of capital, to the tune of 3.5 billion euros. A major surprise was that the nine government-owned German *Landesbanken* passed, though the Hanover-based Norddeutsche Landesbank did so only narrowly. These regional banks were generally considered to be inadequately capitalized. German Finance Minister Wolfgang Schäuble's claim that the test results showed German banks were "robust and resistant" was greeted with, at best, polite disbelief.[236] More to the point, Kenneth Rogoff, professor of economics at Harvard University and a former chief economist at the IMF, defined the European stress tests as "really scary," adding that "we were told everybody is fine; there is nothing to worry about. Now their credibility is less than ever."[237]

Marco Annunziata, chief economist at UniCredit, a major Italian bank, tells the same story in more reserved language: "The overall result seems out of line with the tensions we have been observing in the financial system in the last few months. The tests are unlikely to reassure the market that transparency has been re-established or that pockets of weakness are being rapidly addressed."[238] Peter Hahn, a former Citigroup banker who lectures on finance at the Case Business School in London, noted that "as soon as the political side got involved, people had to question what information would come out, as it became a political exercise rather than a regulatory exercise."[239]

Nicolas Véron, a senior fellow at the Brussels-based think tank Brueghel and a visiting fellow at the Petersen Institute for International Economics in Washington, offers a fundamental explanation for the failure of the European banking stress tests:

> Financial nationalism prevented the tests from being credible or really useful. Nations view the bank tests as a competitive game among countries and not as a way to ensure the common good of European financial

stability…. Any country that restructures its banking system without the neighbors doing the same, runs the risk that parts of its banking industry would be acquired by the neighbors, with no reciprocity.[240]

At least four elements explain why the stress tests were not taken seriously.[241]

- First, the published tests lacked detail, which made it impossible for independent analysts to test the math.
- Second, they only tested for the consequences of a mild downturn in economic activity, not an outright recession.
- Third, regarding the risks related to countries in trouble, such as Greece and Ireland, the tests made a distinction between the so-called "banking book" and the trading book. The banking book includes the bonds and other paper the banks intend to hold until maturity. No possible losses on this portfolio were taken into consideration. Only possible losses on the trading book (i.e., the bonds held for trading purposes) were included in the tests. Not only is such methodology highly questionable, it invites arbitrary composition of both portfolios. Rumors circulated that several major banks had not reported all their holdings of toxic assets.[242]
- Last, the possible losses the banking books might contain in terms of the debt default risks of certain countries were calculated on the basis of risk and failure percentages that were way below what the markets indicated.

The Ghost of Deauville

After the publication of the stress tests, the crisis in the eurozone continued to simmer with no major eruptions. Further downgrades of Spain and Ireland coincided with increasing concerns about the state of the Irish banking sector. The Irish banks included in the stress tests had passed. The Irish banking mess that was about to be revealed in full proved, more than anything else, the irrelevance of the stress tests. The bursting of the Irish real estate bubble weighed heavily on the banks that had financed it with money borrowed short-term on the international money markets.

In 2008, at the height of the crisis, the Irish government had provided a blanket guarantee on all the deposits and most of the debt of the Irish banks. Since then, the financial markets had quite correctly regarded the Irish state and the Irish banks as a single entity. Every banking problem automatically became a public finance issue. The question was not so much if a financial crisis would erupt in Ireland, but when. Ironically, Angela Merkel herself ignited the Irish problem.

On October 18, Merkel and Sarkozy met in Deauville, an old-fashioned, high-class resort town on the coast of Normandy. Under pressure from an increasingly hostile public, Merkel wanted to show that she was prepared to be tough on euro countries with financial problems. The planned European summit of October 28 and 29 was a perfect arena to show her resolve. Given the state of EU politics, a joint French–German proposal seldom meets opposition strong enough to kill it.

At the Deauville meeting, Merkel argued that the German Constitutional Court objected to the ad hoc Greek bailout and temporary rescue mechanisms, such as the EFSF; and that a more permanent rescue mechanism was needed. Merkel also wanted to attach tough conditions to the rescue interventions, but she couldn't get Sarkozy to accept the principle of automatic sanctions. The Deauville agreement went as far as proposing to suspend the EU voting rights of countries that persistently violate eurozone rules.

Merkel also suggested that private bondholders share the pain of any sovereign debt default from 2013 on. This was a watershed event, especially for experienced bond traders. Assurances European policymakers had been giving for months that no eurozone member would be allowed to default suddenly meant nothing. For investors who had not yet started to dump the peripheral countries' bonds, this was the signal to start doing so. As one analyst noted, "Peripheral bonds are credits—you shouldn't look at them as government bonds."[243] Merkel argued that the temporary support scheme devised in May went too easy on private creditors, a view that had widespread support. Her attempt to correct this shortcoming, however, was "spectacularly clumsy."[244]

The Deauville text met with stiff resistance from most of the other eurozone countries. Not only were they displeased by the two major countries once again trying to take the reins, but the proposal to suspend voting rights prompted outright rejections. Even the European Commission president, Portuguese politician José Manuel Barroso, who was not exactly known for courageously standing up to the leaders of the major countries, described the proposal as "unacceptable and, frankly speaking, not realistic."[245] The creation of a permanent rescue mechanism also caused unrest because it implied a revision of the Lisbon Treaty. The general fear was that such a revision might spiral out of control.

The Deauville issues turned the October 28 and 29 meeting into an "ill-tempered summit."[246] Trichet criticized the German-inspired philosophy that rescue operations needed to inflict enough pain on the offenders that they wouldn't commit the same mistakes again in the future. Sarkozy responded by sneering at Trichet that he could not tell politicians what to do. A compromise was finally reached wherein Merkel agreed to a limited revision of the Lisbon Treaty that would create a permanent rescue mechanism and dropped the demand of vote suspension. Article 125 prohibiting bailouts would remain untouched, illustrating the impossibility of transcending the differences of opinion within the European Council. EU President Herman Van Rompuy was given the task of hammering out the specifics of the compromise by the December 2010 summit.

Gaelic Meltdown

Merkel's remark that private bondholders should share in the pain caused by eventual government debt defaults after 2013 continued to resonate in the markets, especially because the conclusion of the October 28 and 29 summit explicitly referred to "the role of the private sector" in the future rescue mechanism as something that needed to be investigated further.

Fear of "haircuts" on existing bonds made markets very nervous and led to a renewed increase in bond spreads for all peripheral countries. Access to market funding became exceedingly difficult. The German insistence on the "bail in" of private bondholders, Greek Prime Minister Papandreou complained, "created a spiral of higher interest rates for countries that seemed to be in a difficult position such as Ireland and Portugal.... It could force economies towards bankruptcy."[247] The Germans, Papandreou cleverly suggested, were deepening and broadening the euro crisis. Van Rompuy fanned the flames when he declared that "we all have to work together in order to survive with the eurozone, because if we don't survive with the eurozone, we will not survive with the European Union." Hardly anyone noticed Van Rompuy's conclusion: "I'm very confident that we will overcome this."[248]

Market unrest focused increasingly on Ireland, the country that had once been known as the Celtic Tiger because of its extraordinary economic growth. The pressure on Ireland intensified significantly after the ECB's two top men, president Jean-Claude Trichet and vice president Vitor Constâncio, hinted that Irish banks could not rely indefinitely on the ECB.[249] By the end of October 2010, Irish banks had 130 billion euros in outstanding ECB loans, almost a quarter of the total liquidity provided by the ECB. On top of these loans, Irish banks were tapping the Irish central bank's exceptional liquidity scheme for no less than 45 billion euros.[250] It's fair to assume that Irish banks were running out of collateral the ECB would accept while big corporate deposits shifted out of the country. Even after massive assistance from the Irish government (pushing the 2011 budget deficit to 32 percent of GDP, or 12 percent excluding the direct consequences of the banking mess), the Irish banks stayed on their feet only with extraordinary amounts of liquidity help from the central banks.

In what was becoming a common ritual in the eurozone, the Irish government pretended it could handle matters without a European rescue package. However, Olli Rehn, the EU's commissioner for economic and monetary affairs, admitted by mid-November that direct negotiations were in process between the Irish government and the IMF and the ECB on the Irish banking situation. As deposits flowed out of the Irish banks at an alarming rate and interest rates rose above 6 percent, Patrick Honohan, the governor of Ireland's central bank, declared on Thursday, November 18 that the government was "definitely likely" to ask for a loan totaling "tens of billions of euros."[251] There was no more denying it: Ireland was the second euro member state to fall to its knees in the sovereign debt.

Over the weekend of November 20 and 21, Ireland officially requested financial assistance. According to finance minister Brian Lenihan, this included "standby facility of a very large sum" rumoured to be 80 to 90 billion euros.[252] On September 20, 2010, Klaus Regling, chief executive officer of the EFSF, had declared in a telephone interview with *Bloomberg News*, "My central scenario is there is no need for the EFSF to become operational."[253] Regling insisted that the sheer existence of the EFSF would be enough to calm the markets. The Irish request demolished the Regling Doctrine.

To avoid offending German sensibilities, the word "bailout" was not mentioned. European finance ministers agreed to Ireland's demand in return for the Irish government's commitment to substantially reduce the budget deficit. Several EMU countries, of which France was the most vocal, urged Ireland to increase its very low corporate tax rate of 12.5 percent. The Irish refused and countered with an overall budget consolidation plan of 15 billion euros over four years. The link between the sovereign debt crisis and the solvency of the European banks was once again made very visible since the rescue package for Ireland was just as much a rescue package for European banks. For example, at that time, German banks had 140 billion euros outstanding in Ireland.

After the Irish rescue operation was announced, concerns arose that Portugal and Spain would follow.[254] In public appearances, politicians showed great confidence that this wouldn't happen. After being asked whether Spain would also have to ask for European help, Spanish Minister of Finance Elena Salgado retorted, "Absolutely not." Portuguese Prime Minister José Sócrates was equally firm: "Portugal doesn't need anyone's help and will solve its own problems."[255] Van Rompuy agreed: "There is no need for help to Portugal."[256]

Markets were not impressed, as bond spreads hardly moved and the ECB seemed to be the only party interested in buying Irish bonds. It did not help Ireland that immediately after the rescue deal, the Green Party, the junior partner in the governing coalition, announced that it would leave the government after approval of the budget in December.

A double-edged doubt dominated in the markets, destroying the hope that the Irish bailout would stop further contagion. On the one hand, hardly anyone believed that the austerity programs would really be carried out. The Greek experience was instructive here. In the slipstream of the bailout decision, Greece took several courageous measures. Greek authorities significantly overhauled

the pension system. Average pensions fell by more than 20 percent, and the retirement age was raised to sixty-five. Civil servants'
salaries were cut by 15 percent, and bonuses were severely limited.
However, protests against these government measures increased
dramatically. During the summer of 2010, violent street protests
culminated in the death of three bank employees. Fearing further
violence, the government and the establishment at large delayed
further reforms. On the other hand, carrying out the programs
would clearly deepen the recession.

Both lines of reasoning intensified the fear of debt restructuring. The markets began to realize that the crisis situation in the
peripheral countries was just the tip of the iceberg. Public finances
in most advanced countries, and certainly in Europe, were out of
control or close to it because of sky-high tax burdens, shrinking
structural growth prospects, mounting pressure to increase expenditures, and the relative aging of the population. Merkel's remark
that "we're in an extraordinarily serious situation as far as the situation of the euro is concerned"[257] was no exaggeration. Her comment was much more on point than the complaint of her finance
minister, Wolfgang Schäuble, who said that the major source of
trouble was the fact that financial markets "do not understand the
euro."[258]

The Talent to Unnerve

The Irish bailout was finalized over the weekend of November 27
and 28 with an 85-billion-euro rescue package, equal to 54 percent
of Irish GDP. Fifty of the 85 billion were destined to bolster public
finances, leaving 10 billion to recapitalize banks and 25 billion
for a contingency fund for the banks. If the Greek rescue was the
death blow to the "no bailout" clause, the Irish one was its burial.
To soften the political fallout, Dublin agreed to contribute 17.5
billion euros to the package. The larger part of this contribution

would come from the National Pension Reserve Fund. It was also decided that no haircut would be imposed on senior bondholders of Irish banks—a decision for which the ECB had pushed especially hard (junior bondholders, however, did suffer major losses). Trichet and company feared that such a haircut would be highly destructive to the still-fragile European bank system.

The European leaders agreed, however, that any future debt rescheduling or restructuring through collective action clauses attached to eurozone government bonds after 2013 would include private creditors. Robert Parker, the chairman of the International Capital Market Association's asset management and investors council, commented that "investors have been led to believe that European government bonds are risk-free and the chance of restructuring is zero. Now investors are being reminded they have to look at sovereign credit risk."[259] Over the same weekend, the EU's finance ministers decided that after 2013, the temporary EFSF would be replaced by a permanent European stability mechanism.

In the week that preceded these decisions, it had become clear that the Irish bailout was not calming the markets. Borrowing costs for peripheral countries reached record highs. Despite Spain's low level of government debt (53 percent of GDP at the end of 2009), markets focused on its high private debt (210 percent of GDP)—particularly its large foreign component. Germany shot down the European Commission's idea to increase the bailout fund, a new manifestation of what Tony Barber of the *Financial Times* described as "the Europeans' distressing talent for fuelling market tensions with imprudent statements and half-formed proposals that unnerve investors and intensify uncertainty about where the euro is heading."[260]

The Economist described Europe's top politicians as the "gang that can't shoot straight," clarifying that "Europe does have leaders who are well drilled in shooting themselves in the foot.[261] Otmar Issing, the main architect of the ECB's initial policies, commented,

"Miscommunication has accompanied Europe's monetary union since the start. The economic crisis, however, has brought forth a Babel of voices."[262]

European leaders demonstrated their distressing talent of making things worse just by speaking out once more when the issue of the stress tests reappeared.[263] Olli Rehn, the European Commission member responsible for economic and monetary affairs, admitted that the earlier stress tests lacked vigor and added that tests to be conducted in 2011 under the authority of the newly created European Banking Authority (EBA) would be more rigorous. This perspective was immediately challenged by some eurozone member states, of which Germany was the most vocal. Markets, unimpressed by the rescue operations that Martin Wolf of the *Financial Times* described as "heroic improvisations,"[264] were so unnerved by these bungled-up communications that by early December, Belgium and Italy had come into focus as possible next victims of Europe's sovereign debt crisis.

Another example of this confusing style of communication emanated from Portugal in early December. Opposition leader Pedro Coelho was the first of the country's political elite to admit that Portugal might need a bailout. Prime Minister José Sócrates forcefully and repeatedly denied that the country needed outside help. The Bank of Portugal, however, claimed that the risks the country was running "will become intolerable if we do not see the implementation of measures that consolidate public finances in a credible and sustainable way."[265]

Three more public examples fed market uncertainty. ECB President Trichet cautiously pleaded for an increase in EFSF funds. Jörg Asmussen, Germany's deputy finance minister, immediately countered.[266] Germany also killed a proposal by Luxembourg's Prime Minister Jean-Claude Juncker and Italian Minister of Finance Giulio Tremonti to launch eurobonds (sovereign bonds jointly guaranteed by all European countries) in an effort to convince the markets and the public of "the irreversibility of the euro."[267] The third example came from Felipe Gonzalez, the former Spanish prime minister, and José Antonio Alonso, the parliamentary leader of the ruling socialist party, who publicly called on the ECB to copy the Federal Reserve's policy of massive quantitative easing—a suggestion Jean-Claude Trichet and other ECB leaders vehemently rejected. The markets kept a close eye on the ECB's immunity to political pressure.

Limited Liability

Markets remained nervous during the final weeks of 2010. A European summit was scheduled for December 17 and 18. In the week before the summit, IMF Managing Director Dominique Strauss-Kahn urged the eurozone authorities "to provide a comprehensive solution to [the eurozone] problem."[268] The Institute of International Finance, a banking lobby organization, released a report estimating that during the year 2011, governments would have to raise $2 trillion and banks $1 trillion to refinance their debt.[269] While the Irish government introduced a courageous budget that included 4 billion euros in spending cuts and 2 billion euros in tax increases, Moody's substantially downgraded the country because its banking problems were so severe. On December 15, violent protests in Athens against the Greek government's austerity measures led to the brutal attack on the street of one former minister.

At the summit, the European leaders confirmed that from 2013 onwards the rescue mechanism would have a permanent character. Although strong German opposition prevented any decision on increasing the size of the fund, Europe's top politicians agreed that the bailout fund would always have the means to rescue any faltering eurozone member. Under German insistence, leaders also agreed that the fund would be subject to national veto and strict conditions. The details would be hammered out in March 2011. Despite political rhetoric, uncertainty reigned about the eurozone's course.

In the financial press, the European authorities' lack of direction came through loud and clear. John Plender of the *Financial Times* summarized it perfectly: "With no shared diagnosis of what is wrong with the workings of the monetary union, still less of what should be done, the future of the union looks uncertain, at best." Irwin Stelzer, former Rothschild investment banker and fellow of the Hudson Institute, claimed, "The Eurocracy responded (to the crisis) with a farcical promise to set up an unspecified structure to raise an unspecified sum to pay an unspecified portion of [the] bills. Germany permitting."[270] Focusing on Germany's crucial role, Wolfgang Münchau of the *Financial Times* concluded that "having prioritised unification in the past 20 years, Germany is now prioritising...the integrity of the eurozone...but not in the same order of magnitude...Germany is now prioritising limited liability."[271]

During the European summit, Trichet gave a presentation in which he criticized the European political authorities' approach thus far as counterproductive, claiming that it had increased market uncertainty.[272] Well aware that certain countries, France among them, favored a much more active role for the ECB, Trichet argued strongly against intensification of the ECB's interventions in the secondary bond markets. The ECB announced at the summit that the member countries' national banks had agreed to increase the subscribed capital of the ECB to 10.8 billion euros. The ECB indicated that this larger capital cushion was needed to cover the risks the central bank had assumed in fighting the crisis. This was not only an admission that the quality of the collateral offered by banks from the peripheral countries was decreasing, it was also a warning that the ECB's role in fighting the euro crisis would cost the politicians.

At the time of the summit, the German Ifo index showed that business confidence in the country was at its highest point in twenty years. Preliminary data on 2010 economic growth showed that Germany, which accounted for about one-third of the euro economy, represented up to three-quarters of the monetary union's economic growth. The days when Germany was "the sick man of Europe" were long gone. This growth was largely export driven, which was good news for Germany's export partners. But the news was troubling for other European countries. Before the monetary union, significant growth in German exports and the accompanying massive trade surpluses would have placed upward pressure on the D-mark, cooling down the export industries. Not so this time around, thanks to the euro. While some countries were dealing with economies that fell like stones and social unrest, the German economy seemed unstoppable.

Just before Christmas, China delivered an early present, or so it seemed. During the third EU–China High Level Economic and Trade Dialogue in Beijing, Chinese Vice Premier Wang Qishan expressed Chinese support for the rescue programs undertaken to support needy eurozone members. In October, Chinese authorities had already offered Greece financial help. The possibility that China might use some of its huge reserves to buy euro-denominated bonds was explicitly linked to Europe's trade policy. The Chinese were unhappy with the way Europe's trade policy had, as Beijing claimed, become more protective toward Chinese products and companies. The EU had already replaced the United States as China's most important export market. A few weeks later it was reported that "Chinese Deputy Prime Minister Li Keqiang reaffirmed Beijing's commitment to continue buying Spanish bonds while he signed off on a number of business deals during a visit to Spain."[273]

Turning to Lisbon, Eyeing Madrid

The vacation markets and investors took during Christmas and New Year's didn't last long, despite Merkel's widely reported speech emphasizing Germany's commitment to the euro. Analysts and economists paid more attention to a paper written by another

German—Otmar Issing, the main architect of the ECB's initial monetary strategy. His essay concluded,

> The nature of Europe has changed with each subsequent institutional development of the community. EMU members may indeed this time back away from substantially reinforcing the rules. In this case, the experience of the first 12 years of EMU teaches us that a new crisis will break out in the not too distant future. Will the community then be under even greater pressure to decide fundamental reform? The present seemingly unstoppable process towards further financial transfers will generate tensions of an economic and especially political kind. The longer this process is characterized by unsound conduct of individual member countries, the more these tensions will endanger the existence of EMU. My conclusion at the start of 2011 is a sombre one. We have not yet reached the moment of truth for EMU. It has merely been postponed.[274]

Europe's sovereign debt crisis was back in the headlines by early January. This time the focus was on Portugal. Only ECB interventions were keeping Portugal's financing costs below 7 percent, a level the Portuguese government had defined as unsustainable. The Swiss National Bank announced that it would no longer accept Portuguese government securities as collateral. Markets worried about Portugal's ability to fund 9.5 billion euros in debt that would mature in April and June 2011. Prime Minister Sócrates kept repeating that Portugal did not need external help: "The country is doing its job and doing it well. Portugal will not request financial aid for the simple reason that it's not necessary."[275] He was echoed by Spanish Minister of Finance Elena Salgado, who claimed that "Portugal will not need a bailout."[276] The fear of further contagion was focused on Spain, but countries like Italy, with its prime minister plagued by corruption and sex scandals, and Belgium, which increasingly looked incapable of getting a new government on its feet, started to show up on the radars.

The authorities responded to fear that the crisis would spread further by promising new stress tests for the banks. The top EU civil servants discussed the need to increase funding to the EFSF and allow it to intervene in the bond markets. The idea of using the fund more as a preemptive measure was also suggested. Olli Rehn, the Finnish EU commissioner for economic and monetary affairs, made these demands public. Writing in the *Financial Times*, he argued that "the effective lending capacity of the current European financial stability facility should be reinforced and the scope widened."[277] Trichet made similar arguments, as did Barroso. However, the Germans shot down the idea, with Wolfgang Schäuble, the most pro-European of Germany's top politicians, describing it as an "artificial debate."[278]

The critical eye of the markets was focused mainly on Portugal, but Spain couldn't get itself off the radar. At 20 percent and still rising, Spain's unemployment rate was the highest in the eurozone. Its economy was in a deep recession and urgently needed structural reforms to increase its growth potential. Spain's financial problems were threefold. First, the saga of the *cajas* continued. The Bank of Spain made public that Spanish banks held 180 billion euros in real estate assets that could turn sour. The largest part of those toxic assets was on the *cajas'* balance sheets.[279]

In mid-January, Prime Minister José Zapatero announced a second round of restructuring for the unlisted *cajas*. Spain had already spent 15 billion euros recapitalizing them, reducing their number along the way, through mergers and closures, from forty-five to seventeen. A further 20 billion to as much as 100 billion euros was needed to adequately recapitalize the *cajas*. Minister of Finance Elena Salgado announced that all Spanish financial institutions needed a minimum core capital ratio of 8 percent of risk-weighted assets by the fall—10 percent for some *cajas*.[280] After intense lobbying, the *cajas* obtained six additional months to do their homework.

The second financial problem for the Spanish government, whose budget deficit was close to 10 percent of GDP in 2010, was the difficulty of keeping the spending of its seventeen regions under control. These regions account for roughly half of Spain's public spending. The debt of the Spanish regions had doubled to 115 billion euros since 2008, not counting the debt of public companies.[281] Regions in Spain were rumored to be significantly underreporting their deficit and debt levels.[282] Social security expenditures also needed to be cut.

At the end of January, the federal government reached an agreement with the unions on a much-needed pension reform. The normal retirement age was increased from sixty-five to sixty-seven, and pensions would be calculated based on income over the last twenty-five years instead of the last fifteen. However, these changes would not be fully phased in until 2027. "Depending on how the economy evolves, we will need another reform sooner or later," commented Spanish economist Pablo Vazquez.[283]

Spain's third financial problem is the huge private sector debt, which amounts to 210 percent of GDP. The overall debt problem, the half-baked pension reform, the stop-go approach to the *cajas,* and substantial wage increases won by the unions—these factors all combined to make it look as if the government wasn't fighting the crisis as energetically as it could. Looming regional elections were clearly affecting governmental decision making. The markets took notice.

"Grand Bargain" Turning "Surreal"

At the end of January, the world's economic elite gathered in Davos, Switzerland for the annual World Economic Forum. European politicians used the occasion to try to convince the world that the euro was safe and that the worst of the crisis was over. Claiming that he also spoke for Merkel, Sarkozy said, "Never, listen to me carefully, never will we turn our backs on the euro, never will we drop the euro…. The euro is Europe…. We will never let the euro be destroyed…. It is not simply a monetary or an economic issue. It has to do with our identity as Europeans."[284] France's minister of finance, Christine Lagarde, claimed that "the eurozone has turned the corner" while Wolfgang Schäuble, her German counterpart, argued, "I don't expect that there will be further major shocks."[285]

Not everyone was impressed by these high-flying remarks from the eurozone's top brass. "If they acted half as tough as they talk, the crisis would be over in days," one European industrial top manager whispered.[286] Larry Summers, who had been secretary of the treasury under Bill Clinton and briefly served as chief economic advisor to Barack Obama, warned that "Europe is testing the limits of reactive incremental strategy…. The laws of economics, like the laws of physics, do not respect political constraints."[287] John Lipsky, the second most important man at the IMF, commented dryly that at the IMF "it was never imagined that under these difficult circumstances, market doubts about the process would dissipate quickly."[288] In line with these critical voices, rumors intensified in Davos that a debt restructuring was becoming inevitable for Greece. Plagued by daily strikes that regularly turned violent, the country seemed to be sliding toward anarchy.[289] Papandreou openly argued in Davos that his country needed more time to pay back its debts. The media hardly noticed when the Vienna Insurance Group, Austria's largest insurer, decided to write down the value of its Greek and Irish bonds by 25 percent.

After Davos, market attitudes brightened, as was evident in the substantial decrease in the crisis countries' spreads over German *bunds.* This optimism was inspired less by the politicians' pep talks than by rumors that a "grand bargain" was in the making. In the days before the February 4 European summit, Merkel visited Barroso, Spanish Prime Minister José Zapatero, and Sarkozy. It soon leaked out that Merkel would be coming forward with a competitiveness pact to improve the eurozone's economic governance.[290] The German chancellor's sense of urgency was related to the political situation in Germany. Increasingly under fire for spending too much German money on undisciplined southern European "budgetary sinners," Merkel faced an electoral catastrophe in several 2011 regional elections.

During the summit, Merkel, firmly supported by Sarkozy, unveiled the "pact for competitiveness." The plan consisted of six points:

1. Abolition of wage indexation
2. Introduction of a common corporate tax base
3. Adjustments to pension schemes in light of the changing demography
4. Insertion of a debt alert mechanism into national constitutions
5. Mutual recognition of educational diplomas
6. Establishment of national crisis management regimes for banks

The pact also included near-automatic fines for offenders. Merkel let it be understood that Germany expected France to accept these rules in return for European access to her country's financial resources. Or, as Irwin Stelzer commented, "Germany will support the financially stricken nations, if they, well, become more German."[291]

However, things did not go as Merkel and Sarkozy had planned. Belgian Prime Minister Yves Leterme commented that "there were eighteen, nineteen countries who spoke up to make known their regret on the way [the Merkel/Sarkozy plan] was presented and also on the content…. It was truly a surreal summit."[292] Not only did the smaller eurozone countries oppose the plan—even Austria, Germany's traditional ally, protested its increase in the retirement age—the European Commission and non-euro EU members protested strongly because they felt sidelined.[293]

Members of the Commission questioned the added value of the pact, which substantially overlapped the Commission's Annual Growth Survey released a few weeks before. Merkel and Sarkozy tried to counter the protests but soon realized they would not win at that summit. Hence, a typically European decision was made: an extra summit would take place early in March during which Van Rompuy would present an adjusted version of the pact for competitiveness. The already-planned summit at the end of March remained on the agenda.

The "surreal" summit of February 4 ended with good news and bad news, although the latter clearly dominated. The good news was that the competitiveness pact signaled growing awareness that, while full political union was nowhere within reach, European leaders knew they needed to work toward that goal to give the monetary union more stable footing. The pact was a step in that direction, as it would potentially bring the EMU closer to an optimal currency area. The bad news was that most of the euro members rejected it. Many governments still refused to yield any part of their policymaking autonomy.

The even worse news was that European leaders still failed to see the immediate crisis. Willem Buiter, chief economist of Citigroup, summarized, "For a number of euro-area sovereigns, the consolidated position of the sovereign and the banking sector looks unsustainable. This means that either the unsecured debt of the banks will be restructured, or the sovereign debt, or both."[294] Or, in the words of Wolfgang Münchau, "A more serious approach to crisis resolution would start with a comprehensive European Union–wide plan to recapitalise and shrink the banking sector. Then, you would restructure whatever sovereign debt needs restructuring."[295]

The Early Morning Surprise
(That Wasn't a Surprise After All)

As one might expect, the summit deadlock made markets nervous again. Spreads, especially on Portuguese bonds, shot up once more, obliging the ECB to strengthen its interventions in the secondary bond market. Additional anxiety-producing factors included European banks' heavy reliance on the ECB liquidity spigot and the ongoing debate over the severity of the planned new stress tests for the European banks. Germany pleaded for weaker standards and less transparency. This uncharacteristic stance stemmed from the difficult situation in which German government-owned regional banks had found themselves.[296]

Wolfgang Franz, chairman of the German Council of Economic Experts, was mainly referring to these regional banks when he said in early 2011, "We don't know what skeletons they still have in their cellars."[297] In addition to the "German problem," the regulators performing the stress tests were in a no-win situation: If they didn't factor in a real sovereign default risk, they would be blamed for ignoring an obvious threat to the banks' solvency. If they did factor it in, any remaining belief that the European authorities could avoid a default would be destroyed.

The attitude of the winners of the February Irish elections didn't exactly contribute to market serenity. They pleaded for a lower interest rate on their rescue package and asked again that senior bondholders of the banks be forced to accept a haircut. Meanwhile, in Germany, France, the Netherlands, and Finland, pressure from skeptical political forces increased substantially. Merkel's own parliamentary majority and the Bundesbank strongly opposed additional funding for the

EFSF and allowing the fund to buy sovereign bonds. One hundred eighty-nine German economists published an open letter stressing the same points.[298] ECB President Jean-Claude Trichet wanted the future permanent rescue mechanism to be able to intervene directly in the bond markets (relieving the ECB from those interventions). With inflation in the eurozone flaring up to 2.4 percent annually, Trichet warned early in March that an interest rate hike in April was inevitable.

Trichet was also quite explicit about the competitiveness pact. In a powerful lecture at the University of Liège in Belgium, Trichet laid out his vision. He went beyond the Merkel and Sarkozy proposals, arguing for stronger surveillance of economic and fiscal policies with automatically imposed sanctions.[299]

Underlining rising international concerns, U.S. Secretary of the Treasury Timothy Geithner visited Berlin a few days before the March 11 European summit to plead for a more comprehensive approach and an enlarged stability fund. When press leaks showed that Barroso and Van Rompuy could only reach a compromise on Merkel and Sarkozy's competitive pact by substantially watering it down, market nerves flared up once again. In the days before the summit, Moody's downgraded Greece to "deep into junk territory...with Athens now considered more likely to default than Venezuela and Argentina, the Latin American outcasts" and Spain to Aa2, two levels below AAA.[300] It was feared that the cost of adequate recapitalization of the Spanish banks could mount as high as 120 billion euros.[301] China's rating agency Dagong downgraded Portuguese debt, and Fitch and Moody's followed suit.

In the early hours of Saturday, March 12, the European leaders surprised the markets and even some within their own ranks by agreeing in principle on some of the important euro crisis issues.[302] They agreed to increase the actual current lending capacity of the EFSF, described by economic historian and Harvard professor Niall

Ferguson as a "giant Ponzi scheme,"[303] from about 250 billion euros to the 440 billion euros originally intended. They also decided that the post-2013 permanent rescue fund, labeled the European Stability Mechanism (ESM), should be able to lend up to 500 billion euros, "likely to be achieved through stepped-up guarantees from triple-A states and paid-in capital from those with weaker balance sheets."[304] However, the credit the ESM would give to troubled countries such as Greece would be senior to the bonds underwritten by private investors (and junior only to IMF debt). This decision was clearly inspired by German refusal to accept the principle of a fiscal transfer union.[305] Direct interventions in the bond markets were ruled out.

Also at the March 11 and 12 summit, Greece and Ireland were offered lower interest rates and longer payback time on their bail-out packages. Greece accepted and agreed in return to sell 50 billion euros of government assets. Ireland refused, since it was asked to give up on its 12.5 percent corporate tax rate.

As for the competitiveness pact, the European leaders agreed only on some general principles. Despite protests from high-debt countries, such as Italy, the leaders agreed to reduce the gap between actual debt levels and the EU's legal debt limit of 60 percent of GDP by 5 percent of GDP each year. Again, however, no unequivocally binding rules were allowed. Coinciding with the summit, Portugal announced new austerity measures to avoid a bailout. Nevertheless, Moody's cut Portugal's sovereign rating to A3.

The *Petit* Bargain

Skepticism about what the March 11 and 12 summit had really delivered soon dominated the markets. Daniel Gros, director of the Brussels-based think tank Centre for European Policy Studies (CEPS) and one of the leading economists on the monetary union, captured the general feeling of disillusionment when he argued that the European Council had "once more decided to kick the can down the road...[failing] to think through the consequences of their actions from the perspective of the markets and [failing] to think through what their decision will mean for the options they will face in the future."[306] Gros concluded that the March agreement "reaffirms a tendency" in European decision making that could be summarized as follows: "No default will ever be allowed, but all bailouts will be preceded by tough talk."

Dark clouds gathered above the upcoming March 24 and 25 summit. First, there was the "Finnish problem." With the prospect of huge gains in the upcoming elections for the highly euro-skeptic True Finns, led by the charismatic Timo Soini, the government of Prime Minister Mari Kiviniemi was not prepared to make a firm decision on the increased funding for the EFSF.

Second, Merkel had lost several regional elections, and the very important election in Baden-Württemberg, Germany's most prosperous state and a long-time stronghold of her own conservative party, was coming up immediately after the summit. Merkel lost the election by a landslide, partly because fears of a nuclear disaster following the tsunami that hit Japan strengthened the Green vote.

Third, just one day before the summit, the Portuguese parliament rejected Sócrates' austerity package, leading to his resignation and making the long-expected bailout of the country unavoidable. Portugal's status was further downgraded, as were thirty Spanish banks. The combined exposure of all the Spanish banks to Portugal was 77 billion euros, by far the largest among European institutions. Luxembourg's Prime Minister Jean-Claude Juncker dismissed the possibility of a domino effect and argued that it "would be absurd for financial markets to target Spain were Portugal to apply for bailout."[307]

The long-awaited Grand Bargain looked grand, but it was *petit* on concrete actions. Two conclusions stood out. First, a limited change in the Treaty on the Functioning of the European Union, to be approved by each member state, allowed the creation of a permanent rescue mechanism "to be activated if indispensable to safeguard the stability of the euro as a whole." The hope was that this phrasing would satisfy the German Constitutional Court.

The permanent European Stability Mechanism (ESM) replaced both the EFSF and the European Stabilisation Mechanism. It would have an effective lending capacity of 500 billion euros, to be acquired through a combination of 80 billion euros of paid-in capital, to be phased in over five years starting in July 2013, and 620 billion euros of callable capital and guarantees from eurozone members. The ESM could only be triggered by unanimous decision of all the ministers of finance. Under very strict conditions, the ESM could buy government bonds in the primary market, but not in the secondary market.

No official decision was made, however, on the effective lending capacity of the current EFSF, except that a compromise would be found by the summer. Neither was private sector involvement in cases of state insolvency clarified. European authorities emphasized that they would adopt the existing IMF procedures for dealing with sovereign debt crises. They failed to clarify the requirement for all euro-area government bonds to include collective action clauses starting in July 2013. The issue of the new bank stress tests was left equally vague.

Recognition was absent that, as Simon Tilford, chief economist at the London-based Center for European Reform, described it,

> we have a banking crisis interwoven with a sovereign debt crisis. Europe needs to address both, and it needs to acknowledge that the banking sector of creditor countries—especially Germany—are not now in a position to handle restructuring and default and that governments will have to pump money into banks to recapitalize them.[308]

The IMF's April 2011 Global Financial Stability Report heavily emphasized the weakness of European banks. European authorities either failed to recognize the effect of undercapitalization of the banking sector on the sovereign debt crisis or avoided the frightening issue altogether. Markets, analysts, and investors had a hard time figuring out which was worse.

Agreement was reached on the Euro Plus Pact (formerly the Pact for Competitiveness or the Pact for the Euro), intended to commit eurozone countries to closer economic coordination to improve competitiveness, increase employment, and reinforce financial stability and the sustainability of public finances. Specific enforcement procedures and sanctions were absent from the pact, which consisted mainly of recommendations. It was further agreed to revise the SGP to enhance the surveillance of fiscal policies. This third version concentrated the surveillance on the debt level as well as the annual deficit and aimed at greater automaticity and more sanctions. But this pact, too, looked more stringent on paper.

Bailout Number Three

At the end of March 2011, the Irish authorities published the results of new stress tests of the Irish banks. The tests found that 24 billion euros in extra capital was needed to revive the banks. The new injection would bring the total cost of propping up the Irish banking sector to 70 billion euros, or almost half the country's GDP. Overall, the markets reacted positively to the test conclusions, despite the fear that the Irish banks would be obliged to turn to fire sales of certain assets, further accelerating price declines. The new Irish government dropped its argument for making senior bondholders bear some of the cost of recapitalization, which contributed to market optimism. The rumor was that the Irish government had given in to pressure from the ECB, where it was feared that such tough talk might cause a eurozone-wide bondholders stampede and renewed problems for the banking sector.

On March 29, Standard & Poor's downgraded Portugal to one notch above junk. A week later, the caretaking Portuguese government asked Europe for help. Portuguese banks were no longer prepared to finance the government's needs, allegedly because the ECB had told them they could not expand their reliance on ECB funding, an action ECB President Trichet denied.[309] The rescue package needed was rumored to be between 70 and 80 billion euros. Markets reacted calmly, despite the prospect of having to hammer out a deal with a caretaker government while an election was approaching. The *Financial Times* commented, "Trouble repaying your debt? Here, borrow some more: How about 80 billion euros? That sums up the eurozone's response to its sovereign debt crisis."[310]

The markets had anticipated Portugal's bailout request. Contagion to Spain was the more immediate fear. Spanish Prime Minister Zapatero had unexpectedly announced in early April that he would not seek re-election. Spanish Minister of Finance Elena Salgado, who three months earlier had explicitly denied Portugal's need for a bailout,[311] now insisted that investors had learned to distinguish between the Iberian neighbors.[312] Salgado "absolutely ruled out" any need for a bailout of Spain.[313] The same message came from José Vinals, the Spanish director of the IMF's monetary and capital markets division: "The actions that have been taken in Spain recently have managed to decouple in the views of markets the fortunes of Spain relative to those of Portugal."[314] The *Financial Times'* Wolfgang Münchau perfectly summarized the situation once again: "European officials quickly pronounced that [Portugal] would be the last rescue ever. Everyone in Brussels fell over themselves to argue Spain would be safe."[315]

However, Spain had major economic and financial problems. The ECB's decision to increase its policy interest rate from 1 percent to 1.25 percent in early April, inspired by the rise in inflation throughout the eurozone, threatened to significantly handicap the country. An estimated 80 percent of Spanish mortgages are set with variable rates. Despite its huge real estate bubble—which was almost as bad as the Irish bubble—real estate prices had not come down much. With more than 1 million properties estimated to be vacant, it was feared that a worsening mortgage debt load might increase not only delinquencies but also pressure for fire sales.

There were three positives in all of this. First, the authorities managed to bring down the budget deficit from 11.1 percent of GDP in 2009 to 9.3 percent in 2010 and projected a 2011 deficit close to 6 percent. Second, even the larger estimates of capital needed to shore up the *cajas* were manageable for the Spanish government debt capacity. Third, the deficit on the current account of the balance of payments was coming down to 3 percent of GDP, easing the country's dependence on foreign capital. In mid-April the Spanish government announced that China would invest 9 billion euros in the *cajas*. Much to Spain's embarrassment, the Chinese authorities promptly denied any such intentions.[316]

The struggling peripheral countries strongly criticized the interest rate increase pushed through by the ECB. But the ECB was in no mood to be intimidated. Increasingly unhappy with the way national and European-level political authorities were handling the crisis, the ECB stopped intervening in the secondary bond market.[317] While decreasing bond spreads factored into this decision, the central bankers also wanted to send a clear message to the politicians. Discussions on the ECB's role in the SMP often overlooked the ECB's financing of the troubled countries through its liquidity-creating mechanisms. With the quality of collateral steadily decreasing, by the end of April the ECB was financing banks in the peripheral countries to the tune of 550 billion euros.[318]

Three events during the second half of April substantially affected the eurozone crisis. First, Timo Soini's True Finns saw a landslide victory in the April 17 Finnish elections. In the days and weeks that followed, the euro-skeptic True Finns kept repeating that "we cannot support the Portuguese rescue package nor the creation of a permanent bailout mechanism."[319] A few weeks later, they pulled out of the government negotiations in Helsinki.

The second event occurred the day after the elections. Standard & Poor's, which had given the United States an AAA rating for seventy years, cut its U.S. outlook from "stable" to "negative."[320] The risk of a future U.S. downgrade exacerbated the overall uncertainty in the bond markets.

Third, as part of a deal on much-disputed French take-overs of Italian firms, Sarkozy endorsed Mario Draghi, governor of the Bank of Italy, to succeed Jean-Claude Trichet, who was set to retire as ECB president by the end of October. Despite deep-rooted German suspicion on all things Italian in terms of monetary stability, Schäuble described Draghi as "the most realistic candidate."[321] Shortly afterward, Merkel openly backed Draghi.[322] Meanwhile, on May 1, Merkel's economic advisor and close aide Jens Weidmann took over from Axel Weber at the helm of the Bundesbank.

Keeping on Ponzi Scheming

While negotiations on the Portuguese bailout package ran their course behind closed doors, the situation in Greece grew more precarious. General opinion held that the Greek authorities couldn't live up to their end of the May 2010 rescue package bargain. The Greek economy remained in the doldrums, with GDP contracting by 4.5 percent in 2010 and again by something like 5 percent in 2011. The budget deficit over 2010 was still 10.5 percent of GDP, and by the end of 2010 total government debt had risen to 143 percent of GDP.[323] Despite optimistic public declarations at the European level and from the IMF, the country was going from bad to worse.[324] Greece's finance minister, George Papaconstantinou, indirectly admitted as much when he declared that Greece would probably not be able to return to the financial markets in 2012 as planned. As roughly 3 billion euros in bank deposits flew out of the country each month, Greek banks had to confront their mounting funding problems.[325]

Analysts and economists increasingly saw a substantial restructuring of the Greek debt as unavoidable, but George Provopoulos, governor of the Bank of Greece, strenuously rejected restructuring of any kind.[326] Shortly after this rejection, the *Financial Times* revealed that plans for a Greek debt failure circulated within the German government. German Deputy Foreign Minister Werner Hoyer declared that a voluntary debt restructuring would "not be a disaster" and that Berlin was ready to back such a plan.[327] EU Commissioner Olli Rehn replied, "We do not see debt restructuring as an option."[328] In early May, the respected German weekly *Der Spiegel* claimed that Greece was thinking about leaving the eurozone,[329] which Greek and European authorities furiously denied. Uncertainty ran sky-high in the markets as, for example, yields on two-year Greek government bonds pushed above 25 percent.

Also in early May, as a new Greek crisis loomed, the caretaking Portuguese government, the EU, and the IMF agreed to a memorandum of understanding whereby Portugal would receive a 78-billion-euro rescue package made up of 26 billion euros from the IMF, and 52 billion euros from the European rescue fund. Of those funds, 12 billion euros were reserved to shore up the Portuguese banking sector, which had become increasingly dependent on ECB funding. The three-year deal would carry an interest rate close to 4.5 percent, half of what the country would have to pay in the markets.

The Portuguese authorities agreed to a reduction of the budget deficit from 9.1 percent of GDP in 2010 to 3 percent in 2013. Public sector pay and pensions were to be frozen until 2013. Several taxes were increased. A 5.5-billion-euro privatizations program was planned. As part of a series of reforms to boost growth and productivity, the minimum wage would be frozen for several years, severance payments would be cut, and unemployment compensation would be reduced. Caretaking Prime Minister José Sócrates remained true to his tradition of shameless drivelling. Not only did he claim to have secured a much better deal than Greece and Ireland, he also insisted that the package would not cause much pain.

"Europe is running a giant Ponzi scheme," read the title of a remarkable and widely circulated *Financial Times* column about the Portugal rescue deal. Its author was Mario Blejer, former governor of Argentina's central bank and director of the Centre for Central Banking Studies at the Bank of England. Blejer witnessed firsthand Argentina's debt default in 2001. He argued that

> the mode adopted to resolve the debt problems of countries in peripheral Europe is, apparently, to increase their level of debt…. The situation resembles a pyramid or a Ponzi scheme. Some of the original bondholders are being paid with the official loans that also finance the remaining primary deficits. When it turns out that countries cannot meet the austerity and structural conditions imposed on them, and therefore cannot return to the voluntary market, these loans will eventually be rolled over and enhanced by eurozone members and international organisations…. [This public sector Ponzi scheme can go on] as long as it is financed with public money…. The constraint is not financial, but political…. [In the end] it will be the taxpayer that foots the bill.[330]

Speaking the Unspeakable

The ink on the Portuguese rescue deal was not yet dry when Jean-Claude Juncker, the prime minister of Luxembourg and president of the eurogroup of finance ministers, declared, "We think that Greece does need a further adjustment program."[331] On top of the May 2010 package's 110 billion euros, Greece would need an additional

30 billion—soon to be revised to 60 billion—to fill its financing gap for 2012–23.

Following the arrest and subsequent dismissal of IMF Managing Director Dominique Strauss-Kahn, who had played a crucial role in the negotiations with the troubled euro countries, the approach to the Greek problem changed. Jean-Claude Juncker lifted the taboo on the word "restructuring" when he contemplated the possibility of a "soft restructuring of Greek debt," while EU Commissioner Rehn suggested the examination of "a voluntary extension of loan maturities, a so-called reprofiling or rescheduling on a voluntary basis."[332]

Both men emphasized that any restructuring was conditional upon Greece stepping up its efforts on tax collection, expenditure cuts, privatization, and structural reforms. The linguistic gymnastics were in part political, but they were also intended to prevent a credit event that would trigger payouts on the credit default swaps (CDS) underwritten to insure against bond defaults.[333] The CDS issue is one more link between the sovereign debt crisis and the banking situation since, according to *The Economist*, "the indications are that investors outside Europe have been net buyers of protection against Greece whereas European banks have been net sellers."[334]

Schäuble, under strong pressure from the majority parties in the German parliament, immediately added that debt rescheduling would necessarily also involve private creditors. The ECB continued to strictly reject any debt restructuring,[335] fearing that it would divert attention from the austerity and reform programs and upset markets. It also wanted to avoid losses on the estimated 45 billion euros in Greek bonds sitting on its balance sheet. Jürgen Stark of the ECB even threatened that "continuation of the liquidity provision [to Greek banks] would be impossible."[336] Greek banks depended on more than 80 billion euros from the ECB (borrowed against Greek paper). "A war is raging over how to solve the Greek debt crisis," Wolfgang Münchau concluded.[337] Subsequent events would prove this statement absolutely true.

Open disagreement among the main parties involved—the ECB, the European Commission, the IMF, and the German government—did not exactly make markets comfortable. This unease translated during the last week of May to new fears of contagion to Spain (where the ruling Socialist Party had suffered a crushing defeat in regional elections), Italy, and Belgium. Bond spreads jumped up again, especially after Jean-Claude Juncker suggested that the IMF might withhold its next payment on the Greek bailout, obliging Europe to increase its own assistance to Greece.[338] The rules of the IMF, which was to provide 30 billion of the 110 billion euros in the Greek bailout program, require that a full-year plan for the financial needs be in place before it can contribute—and it doubted that Greece could fulfill this condition.

Negotiations on a new rescue plan for Greece revealed the extent of the state's failure. The IMF and the European authorities wanted the Greek government to accept direct international involvement in both tax collection and privatization. This prospect increased opposition within the government and within the ruling socialist Pasok Party to Papandreou's policies. Not only would internationally supervised large-scale privatizations threaten their cozy "jobs for the boys [and girls]" networks, money transfers would become much more difficult to organize. In the words of John Sfakianakis, the Greek chief economist of Banque Saudi Fransi, "The Greek political landscape is engrained with vested interests, endemic kleptocracy and bribery. Since the days of Andreas Papandreou, an economist and father of the current prime minister, our politics has been predicated on the expansion of the public sector, patronage and borrowing…. [Papandreou] succeeded in turning his party into the most potent political player, with the unconditional support of trade unions in return for perks."[339]

Attempts at a cross-party consensus in the Greek parliament came to naught, while the streets of Athens rang with public out-cries. Greece's EU commissioner, Maria Damanaki, was first to speak the unspeakable: "The scenario of Greece's exit from the euro is now on the table, as are ways to do this. I am obliged to speak openly.... Either we agree with creditors on a programme of tough sacrifices and results...or we return to the drachma. Everything else is of secondary importance."[340] Spokesmen for the Greek govern-ment vehemently denied the prospect of a return to the drachma.

Damanaki's argument was taken up by Willem Vermeend, professor at the University of Maastricht and Dutch state secretary of finance from 1994 to 2000. Vermeend argued in the top Dutch newspaper that "Greece is broke and should decide for itself that is better to leave the eurozone...the other euro members should en-courage such a move by linking to restructuring and partial cancel-lation of the outstanding debt."[341] Vermeend's plea was published on exactly the same day as a similar argument by Josef Joffe, the editor of the German newspaper *Die Zeit*, in a column entitled "Back to the Drachma."[342]

Simultaneously, Schäuble sounded threatening when he claimed that if Greece would not deliver on the demands of the IMF and the European authorities, "then we will experience what will happen with a currency union if it is not capable any longer to solve its problems."[343] Frank Schäffler of the German Bundestag for the FDP party belonging to Merkel's governing coalition called for Greece "to leave the euro.... [That exit] would not be the end of the euro. It would save the euro."[344] At a party conference of the FDP, one third of the delegates went along with Schäffler.[345]

The Italian Dimension

During the month of June, most of the attention remained fixed on Greece, which, as *The Economist* phrased it, was by now really "teetering on the edge. It is bankrupt."[346] There was no longer any doubt that the country needed substantial additional help in order to avoid bankruptcy. Among the Greek government, the European authorities and the IMF, an unproductive waiting game developed. The IMF only wanted to disburse urgently needed further aid to the Greek government if there was a clear European position on how further to deal with the situation. In turn, the European authorities wanted the Greek government to come up with a new austerity package and measures to improve economic growth and governance first.

Complicating the game enormously was intense disagreement at the European level. This fierce discussion was focused on the insistence among the nations of Germany, the Netherlands, Finland, and Austria that private bondholders also needed to contribute to a new rescue package for the Greeks. The French and the European Central Bank firmly opposed this proposal. ECB president Jean-Claude Trichet stressed again and again: "No credit event, no selective default." At the end of June, Mario Draghi was formally confirmed as the successor in October 2011 to Trichet.

While markets remained in a constant state of nervousness, commentators increasingly sounded pessimistic. Nout Wellink, the governor of the Dutch central bank, argued openly that to save the euro a threefold increase of the resources of the European bailout fund, to 1,500 billion euros, was necessary.[347] Samuel Brittan, the highly respected *éminence grise* among the commentators of the *Financial Times,* wrote that "Greece's euro exit can now only be a matter of time."[348] John Cochrane and Anil Kashyap, two American economists, focused on the broader picture, stressing that while all the attention was focused on Greece "in the end, this is all about Ireland, Portugal, Spain and Italy."[349]

Three influential French intellectuals came to unambiguous conclusions: "The time has come for European politicians to face reality: the euro is dying. It needs to be finished off quickly in order to save the Europeans. But it seems to be appropriate to do it all together in order to avoid a deadly 'every man for himself' scenario ... For France, the benefits of eurozone exit will be immense..."[350] Wolfgang Münchau concluded that "the eurozone is based on three pillars: loopholes, fudges, and lies."[351]

Amidst violent demonstrations in Athens and other Greek cities and after a reshuffle of his cabinet, Greece's prime minister, George Papandreou, was able to obtain in the final days of June Parliament's acceptance of his 28-billion-euro austerity program and 30-billion-euro privatization program. The European Commission concluded that if all this was fully implemented, Greece still needed, on top of the assistance still available from the rescue package of May 2010, at least 85 billion euros of external help to survive the coming three years.[352]

Further stirred up by Moody's downgrade of Portugal to junk and a new interest rate increase by the ECB, markets jumped on Italy early in July after its prime minister, Silvio Berlusconi, attacked his own finance minister, Giulio Tremonti, for the latter's insistence on the need to cut the Italian budget deficit further. Interest rates on Italian government debt and the spread versus the German bond increased substantially.

Tremonti reacted with dramatic words: "If I fall, Italy falls as well.... If Italy, a country too big to be rescued, falls, then the euro falls too."[353] With 1,800 billion in government debt—the third largest in the world—Italy was indeed believed to be too big to be rescued. With Italy under serious pressure, the crisis within the eurozone became existential. Wolfgang Schäuble declared that "the trust crisis, which was evoked by Greece, is now threatening the eurozone as a whole."[354] Sources reported that Sarkozy was informed by his advisors that after Italy's problems, "France is not secure any longer."[355]

With Moody's downgrade of Ireland to junk status and the IMF warning that a "selective default" was becoming unavoidable for Greece, many hoped that publication of the results of the new stress tests performed on European banks would be able to calm the markets somewhat. Of the ninety-one banks tested, nine (five Spanish, two Greek, one Austrian and one German) did not pass the bar, which had been fixed at the conservation of at least 5 percent of tier 1-capital, even under stress. Twelve banks passed the tests by the thinnest of margins. Although they were certainly more solid than the stress tests carried out a year earlier, these new tests did not really impress the markets. The general assessment was that the scenarios being tested were too optimistic, and that the risk of sovereign defaults within the eurozone was largely ignored. Stiff German and Spanish opposition to the tests as carried out by the European Banking Authority did not add to the exercise's credibility.

August Doom

The Italian problems shocked European leaders. Merkel and Sarkozy went into overdrive in order to avoid failure at the European summit of July 21. After some fierce discussion, agreement was reached on two important points. First, a new bailout package for Greece to the tune of 109 billion euros was agreed to.

A third of this sum was to be raised through private sector involvement. Private bondholders were offered four different options, all coming down to bond swaps or rollovers. On a net present value basis, private bondholders were losing 21 percent on their holdings of Greek paper. On the loan component of the new rescue package, the interest was slashed to 3.5 percent and the maturity stretched out to fifteen to thirty years—advantages that were also accorded to Ireland and Portugal.

The second important point of agreement reached on July 21 related to the European rescue fund, the EFSF. The role and the scope of the EFSF were widened. The EFSF was now also allowed to issue lines of credit to countries facing headwinds, to aid in the recapitalization of banks, and to purchase bonds in the secondary market. This enlargement of the EFSF's role inspired Jean-Claude Trichet to drop his stiff resistance to anything resembling a default of Greece (which had now been pretty much decided). European leaders proudly presented the results of the summit and stressed that the aid package for Greece was "an exception" (Sarkozy) and was in any case "the last package" (Juncker).[356]

The July 21 package calmed the markets for just a few days, but soon turmoil returned. It was widely believed that, given the fact that also Spain (with its prime minister, Zapatero, announcing new elections for November) and Italy were now clearly in turbulent waters, the resources of the EFSF needed to be much larger than the available 440 billion euros. Furthermore, the hypotheses underlying the second Greek rescue were quickly defined as unrealistic—particularly with respect to the sums to be raised through privatizations and the timeline for Greece to exit recession.

Most worrisome of all, disagreements among European decision makers soon resurfaced, with most of the criticism coming from Germany. Jens Weidmann, the new president of the Bundesbank, summarized the discontent of many when he argued that the eurozone had taken "a big step towards collectivization of risks … In the future, it well get harder to maintain incentives for sound fiscal policies."[357] Kurt Lauk, president of the economic council of Chancellor Merkel's CDU, warned that there was a real danger that Europe "was rushing into uncontrollable transfer union at great speed."[358]

Analysts at Capital Economics Ltd. spoke for many when they concluded that it is highly doubtful that "the package alone will bring an end to the recent contagion effects and prevents the debt crisis from continuing to deepen in coming months."[359] That deepening happened within days. Driven also by the freaky political

games played in the U.S. on the rise in the country's debt ceiling
(ultimately leading to the U.S.'s downgrade by Standard & Poor's)
and fears of a new recession, markets went haywire early in August. Equity and financial markets in general went through what
the *Financial Times* described as "the worst week since the depths
of the financial crisis."[360] In a panicky mood, Barroso warned that
"tensions in bond markets reflect a growing concern among investors about the systemic capacity of the euro area to respond the
evolving crisis."[361]

Over the weekend of August 6 and 7, Sarkozy, Merkel, and
Trichet tried to turn the tables. Merkel and Sarkozy pledged that
the conclusions of the July 21 summit would be turned into national law before the end of September. Merkel firmly refused to
consider the introduction of eurobonds. In return for theis pledge
made by Sarkozy and Merkel, Trichet agreed to intensify the ECB's
purchases of bonds of troubled euro countries. The ECB acted ac-
cordingly and succeeded in lowering the spreads on Spanish and
Italian bonds. Yet the overall market uneasiness did not disappear.
When rumors started to circulate that France might also be losing its AAA rating, uncertainty increased. A woefully inadequate
budget package announced by the French government on August
24 didn't help either.

During the remaining weeks of August, opposition to the
July 21 package increased in Germany, the Netherlands, Finland,
Austria and Slovenia despite the proposal made by Merkel and
Sarkozy to form an economic government for the eurozone. German president Christian Wulff openly questioned the legitimacy
of the ECB's bond buying program, while the Bundesbank also
intensified its campaign against the ECB policies. Finland tried
unsuccessfully to negotiate a deal with Greece for the provision of
specific collateral for Finland's part in the second rescue package of
Greece. While economic growth further nosedived and American

money market funds increasingly withdrew funds from Europe, the problems inside the European banking sector again took center stage. The ECB had to once again increase its emergency lending on behalf of the banks. Christine Lagarde, the new director general of the IMF, declared the European banks to be in need of substantial injections of fresh capital, thereby discrediting the results of the recent stress tests performed on the European banks. The problem for many European banks was not only insufficient capital but also a lack of a stable funding base. In Greece, where the recession further intensified, the second and third bank of the country, Alpha Bank and Eurobank EPG, faced mounting funding problems and finally merged.

The manuscript of this book was finalized on August 30, 2011. Amidst the extraordinary uncertainty surrounding the future of the euro and the European monetary union, one thing seemed to be unmistakably true: This crisis is far from over. A frighteningly volatile summer will be followed by a hot fall, and still more turbulent seasons after that. Although the battle lines are clearly drawn and the issues to be resolved are there for everybody to see, the final outcome is still far from clear. In the next chapter, the possible scenarios for the future are developed. In each of them, the attitude and positions taken by Germany will be decisive. Odds are that Germany will distance itself increasingly from the euro project, with a German exit from the eurozone becoming increasingly likely.

There is, however, much more at stake than just the continuation of a monetary union. The more uncertain the future of the euro becomes, the greater the risk that the whole project of European economic integration will unravel. This prospect has already powerfully been evoked by, among others, European president Herman Van Rompuy. Otmar Issing, the intellectual father of the ECB and a man widely appreciated for his moderate judgments, also showed great concern. He wrote that the way in which the crisis in the eurozone was handled by the authorities threatened to lead to "the collapse of the most successful project of economic integration in the history of mankind."[362]

Chapter 4

The endgame (it's all in Germany's hands now)

HE FIRST DECADE OF THE EMU AND THE EURO WAS generally considered a resounding success. The euro's launch went off without a hitch, and the ECB outperformed predictions. The EMU and the euro sailed a debt-fueled stream of economic growth and rising employment. A massive supply of goods from China and other emerging economies kept inflation down. However, problems and imbalances lurked beneath the surface, hidden by the booming world economy. Inflationary bubbles began to surface in different asset categories. Some of these bubbles were astronomical in size (e.g., housing in Ireland and Spain). Kenneth Dyson, professor in the School of European Studies at Cardiff University, claimed the eurozone "had the reward of a lucky early life. However, it was simmering potentially multiple crises."[363]

The financial crisis of 2007–09 and the accompanying recession pushed the eurozone's structural problems into the spotlight. The crisis really got going by late 2009, when the Greek government admitted that its accounts had been thoroughly falsified and its public finances were a mess. The ECB's active engagement in the secondary bond market and the creation of the European Financial Stability Facility (EFSF) temporarily calmed the markets.[364]

It soon became clear, however, that the crisis management of the European authorities was lacking a sense of urgency and fraught with inconsistencies, moral hazard issues, and different lines of interpretation. A new crisis broke out toward the end of 2010 with Ireland claiming center stage. Portugal followed Ireland down the bailout path in the spring of 2011. By then, a second bailout of Greece had become inevitable.

Greece's slide into ungovernability and chaos was visible to all,[365] but the peripheral countries were trapped in a policy approach that focused solely on lending money against promises of austerity and structural reforms. The contradictions inherent in this approach turned this precarious situation into a highly destructive cycle. As the crisis progressed, incoherence, lack of courage, and short-sighted nationalistic reflexes added to the problem. Wolfgang Münchau of the *Financial Times* hardly exaggerated when he referred to "the serial incompetence of the eurozone's decision-makers."[366]

As the crisis deepened, experts increasingly started to warn for the breakup of the monetary union. Many analysts, commentators, and policymakers disagreed. The union was not in danger, policymakers claimed. Of course, the question then becomes: What does the future of the EMU and the euro *really* look like? This question can only be answered in terms of scenarios with varying degrees of probability. In the coming section, I develop three such scenarios and label them *More Of the Same* (MOS), *Throwing Out the System* (TOS), and *Rebuilding Of the System* (ROS).

MOS: The Basics

In this scenario, the authorities involved in the crisis within the eurozone—basically national governments and regulatory bodies, the European Central Bank (ECB), the European Commission (EC), and the International Monetary Fund (IMF)—persevere with the policies they followed during the first year and a half of the crisis. This approach, largely improvised as the crisis unfolded, was essentially built on two tiers.

The first consisted of simply throwing more credit at the problem. A major catalyst for this approach came from the fear that an outright default of one or more of these countries would ignite a new banking crisis. The claims of European banks on the troubled euro member countries are substantial. All European banks combined had at the end of March 2011 a sum of close to 2.2 trillion euros outstanding on the five PIIGS-countries (see **Table 4.1**). Citigroup economists Willem Buiter and Ebrahim Rahbari correctly claimed that "the choice faced by the French and German authorities in particular is to either bail out Greece or to bail out their own banks."[367] This argument can be extended to Ireland, Portugal, and also Spain and Italy. Stress tests of the European banks were carried out with such a blatant lack of seriousness that they fueled market uncertainty instead of reducing it.[368]

The money reached Greece, Ireland, and Portugal via two channels. The more visible channel was the bailout programs, where money contributed to the EFSF by the national governments of the EU or EMU members[369] was combined with credit made available by the IMF. The sums raised in this way meant an extra fiscal burden for all the countries concerned and a further risk to their credit ratings.[370]

The second and less visible (but very real) channel was credit flowing from the ECB, not only to the banks in Greece, Ireland, and Portugal, but also to other countries, such as Spain and Belgium. The ECB money machine also ran on two propellers. Besides extending credit lines against these countries' collateral (mainly bond and other treasury paper issued by the governmental authorities), the ECB also intervened in the secondary bond market, buying bonds of the same troubled countries. In mid-2011, the ECB made roughly 210 billion euros available to Greece, Ireland,

Table 4.1 Bank exposures (1)

ON	CLAIMS OF		
	All Euro-pean banks	German banks	French banks
Greece	128	24	57
Portugal	205	39	28
Ireland	378	116	30
Spain	637	178	146
Italy	819	165	410

Source: BIS

(1) in billion $ at the end of March 2011

and Portugal through the credit line mechanism and 75 billion euros through its targeted bond purchases. An estimated 45 billion of the 75 billion euros went to Greece.[371] The ECB defended its acceptance of inferior collateral with the argument that the creditworthiness of the countries concerned remained basically intact as long as official bailout money remained available to them.

The second tier of policy was made up of the so-called conditionality, being the austerity and reform programs negotiated with or, perhaps more accurately, imposed on the peripheral euro countries. The dire state of the public finances in each country meant urgent action was essential to prevent government debt from becoming unsustainable. Hence, governments were pushed to cut spending and increase taxes to put their fiscal houses in order and decrease their reliance on foreign capital.

This action was also needed to bring down the excessive reliance of these countries on foreign capital. The deficit on the current account of the balance of payments measures the reliance on foreign capital. For that reliance to diminish, it is essential that internal spending is brought more in line with internal production. Cuts in government expenditures are imposed in order to reduce spending.

The reform programs imposed on these countries aim to raise these countries' production and growth potential by improving efficiency and productivity. Because implementing these reforms in product and labor markets often means going against special interest groups such as unions and protected industries and companies, they often carry immense political difficulties. In Greece (more so than in Ireland or Portugal), the task of pushing through the reforms in the context of recession, internal devaluation, and pessimistic expectations proved to be an uphill fight. This is one of the major reasons Greece quickly needed a second bailout program.

MOS: The Ponzi Option

To pull the peripheral countries out of the crisis, higher-level, long-term economic growth is needed. The spending cuts and tax increases are only a short-term solution. What's more, wages have to be forcefully restrained or even cut to restore international competitiveness. The loss of international competitiveness for Greece, Ireland, Portugal, and even Spain and Italy was substantial. Because joining a monetary union means giving up the policy lever of currency devaluation, the only option left to restore international competitiveness is an internal devaluation focused on wages. However, in the long run, even a successful internal devaluation decreases incomes and hence the burden on consumers and producers, restricting consumption expenditures and investments.

Furthermore, the downward pressure on wages exacerbates the deflationary tendencies that emanate from the spending cuts and tax increases. As a consequence, the recession deepens and unemployment increases. The increasing interest on the fast-growing outstanding debt pushes the government into budget deficit. A shrinking GDP increases the debt ratio on its own. External demand normally softens the impact of internal deflation, but improving international competitiveness through wage cuts takes time. Countries seem to vary in their ability to push wage cuts through, however; Ireland was able to improve its international competitiveness fairly quickly, while the other peripheral countries had more difficulty.

With the possible exception of Ireland, none of the troubled countries can achieve high enough growth levels to substantially reduce the deficit and stop the public debt from escalating. The harder they try, the deeper into recession they fall and the greater public discontent grows with the policies pursued. Under such circumstances re-election becomes impossible, as Ireland and Portugal demonstrated in the first half of 2011. Backed into a corner, politicians try every trick in the book to free themselves from the policy trap. If they succeed, they find themselves in a Catch-22 as deficits escalate and structural reforms are postponed, deepening the crisis.

It does not help that the world economy is not exactly in a phase of intense growth. As the Greek experience showed, a troubled country needs more loans to stay afloat, which restarts the charade: the government negotiates new reform measures and those who need to come up with the money put on their tough acts. Things go from bad to worse because demand is insufficient to keep the economy going and too many fundamental problems remain unresolved, or even worsen. While Greece has suffered most publicly, the same forces are at work in Portugal. Ireland's growth perspective is somewhat less bleak given its improved international competitiveness and its better investment and entrepreneurial climate.

The mechanisms behind the MOS scenario can technically keep going almost indefinitely because they run on public money. With the ECB's cooperation, the supply of public money can be made quite elastic. New debt is piled on old debt, and existing credit lines are extended. This is where, as economist and former governor of the Argentinian central bank Mario Blejer first described it,[372] the whole European policy approach turns into a Ponzi scheme. But whereas a Ponzi scheme based on private money collapses as soon as trust is lost, one built on public money can go on until national authorities refuse to keep the money and credit flowing toward the countries in need.

The risk of such a refusal became evident with the first bailout packages. It originated in the richer, more frugal Germany, the Netherlands, Austria, and Finland. Public outrage over policymakers' decision to throw taxpayers' hard-earned money at countries behaving so irresponsibly makes it impossible for the funding to continue.[373] Continuing to lend to the troubled countries would eventually result in complete fiscal union for the eurozone, an option that is unacceptable to several countries, specifically Germany. Pressure to go down this road may at some point trigger a German exit from the monetary union.

Also important with respect to politicians' refusal to go on with the MOS policies is the faith of the ECB. An independent central bank is part of Germany's national DNA. Politicians who participate in a complete politicization of the ECB are bound to be punished severely in the next election. Such politicization, however, is the inevitable outcome of several more years of the MOS policies. As the MOS scenario unfolds, public protests and downgrading by rating agencies quickly limit politicians' abilities to raise more money from their own budgets. As history has shown, erosion of the independence of the central bank is certain in such circumstances.

MOS: Accelerators

At some point, policymakers who use the MOS approach are obliged to contemplate debt restructuring. However, debt restructuring does not fundamentally improve the troubled countries' prospects. Debt restructuring can take various shapes, and policymakers do their utmost to hide the true extent of their restructuring plans. As Simon Tilford of the Centre for European Reform has argued, even a haircut of 50 percent of the outstanding debt will not solve the problems of countries like Greece and Portugal, basically because of two elements.[374] First, a haircut in itself does nothing to improve international competitiveness. Hence, the countries' growth prospects are basically unchanged.

Second, the contribution of even such a drastic cancellation of debt to the annual government budget through reduced interest payments would still be largely insufficient to eliminate the deficit on the budget. During 2011, interest payments will amount to 5.8 percent of GDP for Greece, 3.9 percent for Portugal, and 3.3 percent for Ireland. For comparison, interest payments for 2011 will amount to 4.9 percent of GDP for Italy, 3.5 percent for Belgium, and 1.6 percent for Spain.[375] Suppose for the sake of argument that by the time a default with a 50 percent haircut is organized, interest charges have gone up to 8 percent of GDP for Greece and 6 percent for Portugal and Ireland. A 50 percent reduction would then reduce the budget deficit by 4 percent for Greece and 3 percent for the two other countries. The OECD predicts 2011 budget deficits of 7.5 percent for Greece, 5.9 percent for Portugal, and 10.1 percent for Ireland, estimates that were almost immediately recognized to be somewhat on the rosy side.[376] The reduction in interest burden following a haircut of even 50 percent would be most welcome, but it wouldn't reduce the need to follow deflationary policies.

The MOS scenario can continue for several years, but eventual failure is inevitable. This is true for Greece, Portugal, and probably Ireland as well. The end will come, as explained earlier, when one of the richer countries refuses to put up money. Of course, Greece, Ireland, and Portugal are very small economies; together, they make up only 6.1 percent of the eurozone's total GDP.[377] As the euro crisis continues, uncertainty surrounding the project grows among consumers, producers, investors, and most significantly, financial markets. However, if other countries choose the bailout path, the crisis will escalate savagely.

The first country that comes to mind when thinking about contagion is, of course, Spain. Faced with depression-like unemployment, a shaky banking sector (especially the *cajas*) and regional authorities undermining federal efforts to fix the hole in the government budget, Spain represents 11.5 percent of the eurozone GDP, close to double the share of the three smaller troubled countries *combined*. In the words of Paul Krugman: "The others are tapas, Spain is the main course."[378]

Not far behind Spain are Italy (16.8 percent of the euro-GDP), Belgium (3.8 percent of the euro-GDP), and even France (21.2 percent of the euro-GDP). Italy and Belgium already face high public debt (but, luckily, relatively low private debt) and government instability.[379] The French budget situation is worse than most people realize. Not only did the country only respect the 3 percent limit on the budget deficits in five of the thirteen years since the monetary union started, its outstanding debt rose from 70 percent of GDP in 2006 to 100 percent in 2011 (compared to 65 percent and 84 percent, respectively, for Germany).[380] In almost any exercise on intergenerational accounting, France is among the worst-performing European countries.[381]

However, the MOS approach can end sooner through either of two other developments. The first is a serious crisis in the European banking sector. Anil Kashyap, Kermit Schoenholtz, and Hyun Song Shin, three respected scholars on the banking industry, summarized the issues involved here as follows: "Insufficient capital, combined with volatile financing, makes the European banking system prone to a run.... In Europe, some banks have turned increasingly to borrowing from the ECB, while paying higher premiums to borrow in private markets to compensate for their risk of default.... Ultimately, the crisis in Europe will continue until we have answers to two critical questions: How much money is needed to stabilize the banks, and where will it come from?"[382] The longer an MOS policy is followed, the higher the risk the European banking sector runs of getting caught in a crippling crisis.

The other development that might accelerate the demise of the MOS policy is the descent of one or more of the troubled countries into chaos, anarchy, and complete ungovernability. By the summer of 2011, Greece was almost there. The austerity programs and internal devaluation imposed on Greece could lead to the collapse of democracy. Rigid adherence to MOS policies risks sending other countries down the Greek road. In the words of Norman Lamont, the British chancellor of the exchequer from 1990 to 1993, "The real problem is that the only way that countries like Greece and Spain and Portugal can regain their competitiveness with Germany is to impose a decade of restrained living standards on their populations. That is the time bomb ticking inside the euro."[383] If one or more countries descend into real chaos, the only certainty is that MOS policies will go out the window.

TOS, or Doing a Tango

One way out of the MOS option is the approach that throws out the system (abbreviated to TOS), meaning that countries choose to exit the monetary union as the least bad option available. Greece, the country in the deepest mess, would obviously be the first candidate to go down this road. If the policies followed during the first year and a half continue, TOS will also be the only option left to Portugal and Ireland. Such an exit would improve these countries' international competitiveness overnight.[384] It would immediately improve their growth prospects, since the value of the new national currencies would immediately go down versus the euro and other currencies.

But is this a realistic option? Aren't the costs involved so huge that an exit would be more costly than any of the other policy options? If European policymakers have been consistent on any point during the crisis, it is their rejection of any country's exit from the eurozone. A practical look at two precedents, Argentina and Iceland, is instructive.

Argentina's economy moved from chaos and hyperinflation in the 1980s to single-digit inflation in the 1990s.[385] This achievement, remarkable in a Latin American context, was mainly due to the adoption of a currency board arrangement that wrote into law that the value of one Argentinian peso would always be equal to one U.S. dollar. Just as countries in Europe would join the eurozone, Argentina joined the dollarzone. This arrangement eliminated the Argentinian central bank's monetary policy autonomy (as it did for countries accepting the euro). At first, the resulting monetary stability and credibility brought major benefits to the Argentinian economy and society. In striking similarity to the experience of peripheral eurozone countries during the first years of the EMU, low interest rates boosted internal demand and the prospect of stability attracted foreign funds, rapidly leading to an escalating foreign debt.

However, as happened in the eurozone, Argentina ignored the lessons it could have learned from the theory of optimum currency areas (OCA). The Argentinian authorities forgot the necessity of budgetary discipline and neglected to create flexible and mobile labor markets that could cushion the economy when shocks hit. By the mid-1990s, tensions were building in the form of rising debt levels, excessive current account deficits, and a gradual loss of investor confidence. The Brazilian devaluation of 1998 exacerbated Argentina's growing problem of international competitiveness.

The Argentinian authorities had to call in the IMF for financial assistance. The IMF imposed an austerity program that led to violent riots and a deep political crisis. Argentinians took their money abroad—sometimes literally, in their luggage. With the country's back against the wall, the dollar link was cut in January 2002, the currency devalued by 70 percent against the dollar, and holders of Argentinian bonds had to accept a haircut of 65 percent. Inflation went up to 26 percent in 2002, coming down to 13 percent and 4 percent, respectively, in the two following years.

This burst of inflation took care, so to speak, of the most pressing aspects of the internal debt mountain. After contracting by, on average, 3 percent a year from 1999 to 2001 and even 11 percent in 2002, the real economy rebounded in China-like fashion with an average growth rate of 8.5 percent from 2003 to 2008. Booming exports, growing by 15 to 20 percent in the years after 2002, drove the economic expansion. The surplus on the current account of the Argentinian balance of payments was, on average, 3 percent of GDP per year over the same period. Public debt went down to 40 percent of GDP. The Argentinian economy was among the strongest performers worldwide after the recession of 2009.

However, the drastic policy change carried a cost. "In the seven years following the devaluation," Uri Dadush and Bennett Stancil argue, "the total cost of default to foreigners, including the direct cost of lost principal and interest and the indirect losses in equity values, has been estimated to be nearly twice as large as the initial value of the debt in default."[386] Argentina had cornered its creditors and obliged them to take a severe hit to create breathing space for its economy. A decade later, the thrust of international investors has not yet returned. Argentina's credit rating remains very low and its access to the capital markets is still limited.

Greece or Portugal, and to a lesser degree Ireland and even Spain, have much in common with Argentina at the start of the twenty-first century: a total loss of international competitiveness, public finances in disarray, public debt rising to unsustainable levels, a too rigidly organized economy incapable of healthy economic growth, widespread capital flight, huge current account deficits, and complete loss of investor confidence. Greece in 2011 is in even worse shape than Argentina was in 2001.[387] Steps like those Argentina took are inevitable for Athens.[388] The same argument holds for Lisbon, with Dublin not far behind (and Madrid also in sight). But let there be no mistake: TOS is not really a good option. It is the least bad of a limited number of options available.

TOS, or Going Icelandic

Iceland's experience is at least as instructive for Greece and the other troubled eurozone countries. It is hard to think of a country that was hit harder by the financial crisis than thinly populated Iceland. "Iceland has experienced one of the deepest financial crises in modern history," according to Mark Flanagan, IMF mission chief for Iceland from 2008 and 2010.[389]

Without a doubt, the crisis was, to a large extent, of the country's own making. The authorities allowed the Icelandic banks to grow entirely out of proportion. The banks, especially the big three—Kaupthing, Glitnir, and Landsbanki—grew so large their assets equalled ten times the country's GDP.[390] They fueled a credit boom without precedent and an equivalent housing bubble. At the height of the collapse in late 2008, it looked as though the country was on the verge of financial and economic extinction. It was saved from complete bankruptcy in November 2008 by a hastily negotiated IMF standby assistance program.[391]

Just like Argentina at the end of 2001, Iceland found itself with its back against the wall. While Greece and the other troubled eurozone countries could fall back on the support provided by the big brothers of the euro family, Iceland was on its own. However, being alone out there in the freezing cold turned out to be a major advantage. Asgeir Jonsson, a professor of economics at the University of Iceland, wrote,

> Iceland's luck was that it did not qualify for a bailout.... Europe's bailout path has only diverted ever-more re-

sources to failing enterprises, postponing and deepening the problem. Iceland's restructuring was both painful and costly for the population, but the government did not throw good money after bad, and the taxpayers were spared a nationalization of private debts.[392]

Drastic measures were indeed taken.[393] The Icelandic authorities recapitalized the domestic banking sector but let foreign operations go bankrupt.[394] The banking recapitalization led to a huge budget deficit that was further increased by a number of measures taken to stop the mind-boggling fall in aggregate demand. From a surplus equal to 5.4 percent of GDP in 2007, the budget jumped to a deficit of 13.5 percent in 2008, one of the most massive budget position changes any OECD member state had experienced in such a short interval.

Government debt, standing at a healthy 53 percent of GDP in 2007, almost doubled to 102 percent at the end of 2008. The economy contracted by more than 10 percent (–6.9 percent in 2009 and –3.5 percent in 2010). The unemployment rate more than doubled from 3 percent in 2008 to 7.5 percent in 2010. The inflation rate peaked at 19 percent on an annualized basis, and the current account deficit rose to a breathtaking 25 percent of GDP in 2008.

The Reykjavik government installed rigid capital controls, organized sensible schemes to help families and corporations deal with their distressed balance sheets, and let the krona devalue between the end of 2008 and the end of 2009 by 40 percent, after which it stabilized. Together with sustained wage moderation, the currency devaluation substantially improved the country's international competitiveness. Unsurprisingly, exports increased in volume by close to 10 percent over 2009–10, despite the deep recession in the rest of the Western world. The increase in external demand allowed the government to cut expenditures and increase taxes.

As a result, the budget deficit was cut to 2.7 percent of GDP in 2011, the year the Icelandic economy expanded by 2.2 percent. Iceland's finance minister, Steingrimur Sigfusson, modestly declared in April 2011 that his country could "amaze the world with a speedy and good recovery."[395] Signaling international approval for Iceland's remarkable turnaround, in June 2011 the country was able to raise the intended 1 billion dollars through its first international bond offering in the open market. With a five-year duration, the bond's interest rate came out at just below 5 percent, a rate of which troubled euro members could only dream.

As was true with Argentina, the default-and-devaluate solution did not solve all of the Icelandic economy's problems. Authorities still struggle with the lifting of the capital controls, the stubbornly high unemployment (by Icelandic standards), the high level of government debt, the need to further restructure the banking sector, and the still impressive external deficit, among other issues. However, it's undeniable that although Iceland was hit much harder by the financial crisis, the policies its authorities followed brought about an economic turnaround that surprised everybody, including private and public macroeconomic forecasters.

Serious analysis of the Icelandic crisis supports the importance of quick and decisive action on all fronts and the crucial role of currency devaluation. Countries that step out of the euro will need to implement capital controls and recapitalize their internal banking sectors. To avoid a prolonged ban from the international capital markets, the default on outstanding debt must be carefully negotiated with the parties involved. Perhaps most important, to get a broad majority of the population on board, policymakers and authorities should tell their audiences the truth about the situation and how they are dealing with it.

ROS, or Back to Square One

Is TOS really a sensible policy option for Greece and the other distressed euro members? The experiences of Argentina and Iceland suggest so it may be so. The MOS approach carries even greater costs, both for the troubled countries and for the eurozone as a whole. Of course, as Argentina and Iceland show, following the TOS approach means taking a number of painful measures simultaneously. But MOS will eventually necessitate the same measures, and with no light at the end of the tunnel. Despite its costs, TOS at least offers hope.

Would an exit of one or more members of the eurozone eventually cause the monetary union to end? The fear is that once a country drops out of the euro, speculators will immediately look for the country most likely to follow suit. When the second victim falls, the hunt for the third begins, and so on. This fear is unfounded as long as two conditions are met. First, if the exit is organized and executed well, markets will realize that the country's future prospects have brightened considerably and that the eurozone's viability has improved.

Second, market behavior will turn negative if the eurozone takes no follow-up action. This further action is needed on two broad fronts. First, a cleanup and recapitalization of the banking sector needs to be engineered. Second, and most important of all, institutional adjustments must be made to bring the union more in line with the prescriptions of the theory of optimum currency areas. This argument brings us back to square one.

Smooth and efficient functioning of a monetary union depends on the fulfillment of certain conditions. Four of these conditions are not met (or not fully met) in the eurozone: political union, fiscal integration, labor mobility, and price and wage flexibility. The crises in the peripheral countries exemplified the consequences of leaving these conditions unfulfilled but also demonstrated the problematic nature of policy initiatives taken to fill the gaps.

From Indifference to Opposition

If the EMU is to survive, its shortcomings and inconsistencies must be corrected. Even if the weaker countries leave the union, the remaining countries will still need to rebuild the system along more sensible lines. Are policymakers up to the task? Are the European people ready to support their leaders in this endeavor? The answer to both these questions is likely no.

In January 2007, almost a year before the international financial crisis and three years before the crisis in the eurozone, more than half of the citizens of Germany, France, Italy, and Spain felt that the euro was negatively affecting their national economies.[396] Such negative feelings only increased as the crisis unfolded. Large segments of the populations of the rich, AAA-rated northern countries—Germany, the Netherlands, Finland, Austria, and Luxembourg—resent using their hard-earned wealth to help the undisciplined peripheral countries.[397] Since Germany is by far the most important economy within the eurozone and the one with the deepest pockets, the German people's attitude is a crucial determinant of the monetary union's future.

In the peripheral countries, the attitude toward Europe and the euro used to be rather positive. The people's first reaction to the crisis was to blame their own political leaders. But when they realized how much pain the austerity programs caused, they refocused their anger on Europe and the euro. Ordinary citizens associated the idea of a unified Europe with more taxes, reduced services, more unemployment, and even outright poverty, not to mention the humiliation of national pride.

In most EU countries, a small political and economic elite had always been the main proponents of monetary union and European integration in general. As the havoc and misery caused by often violent conflicts between European countries became a distant memory, most Europeans became increasingly indifferent. Monetary union didn't help much, they felt, but it didn't hurt, either. So when the project did start to hurt, unsurprisingly people quickly and sharply turned against it.

Powerful interest groups started to have second thoughts as well. Labor unions, protected professions, nationally shielded sectors, and corporations all began to take a more negative view of the unification project as it eliminated their privileges. Masters of disguising their self-interested motives, these groups strengthened public unease with the euro through their powerful rhetoric.

Vote Maximizers

Obviously, politicians factor public opinion into their decision making. The increasingly negative attitude toward Europe and the euro made it difficult for national leaders to defend pro-European policies and intervention. Politicians had more to contend with than just hostile public opinion, however. The monetary union has fundamentally altered the political environment in the member countries.

Many European politicians, consciously or unconsciously, have taken an ambivalent attitude toward EMU and the euro. On one hand, monetary union has economic and political advantages. On the other hand, it limits the political autonomy of member countries. As Luxembourg's prime minister, Jean-Claude Juncker, recognized in January 2008, "politicians are vote maximisers.... For the politician, the euro can render vote-maximising more difficult, as a smooth and frictionless participation in the monetary union sometimes entails that difficult decisions have to be taken or that unpopular reforms have to be initiated."[398]

The first and most significant change EMU brought about was that the ECB took responsibility for monetary policy within the whole eurozone. ECB statutes stipulate that the institution is largely independent of the political authorities. The crisis was a heavy blow to this independence. But even before the crisis, French and Italian politicians in particular found it difficult to hide their frustration with the ECB. They felt that the ECB's monetary policy obstructed their domestic agendas. But national frustration with the consequences of a European monetary policy is only the beginning of the story.

In the slipstream of the euro crisis, economists and analysts agree almost universally that closer political and fiscal union and strict and enforceable limits on member countries' budgetary freedoms are needed to ensure the euro's survival.[399] In the words of Simon Tilford, "A fiscal union will be essential to the eurozone's survival. But the obstacles to such fiscal supranationalism are daunting. The crisis has cruelly exposed the limits of solidarity between the member states."[400]

The so-called structural policies, such as the Europe-wide implementation of competition law and the deregulation of the labor, energy, and telecommunications markets, further limit the options for national politicians. At the least, these policies will require interventions that clash with short-term electoral considerations. Unfortunately, the nature of politics makes it difficult to transcend this type of short-term thinking.

A Herculean Task

Because a well-functioning monetary union limits their freedom, politicians find it more difficult to maximize their share of the votes. The iron law of politics is that politicians without votes are irrelevant. As Hans Tietmeyer explained in 1996, "Monetary union means a restriction on national sovereignty, on national manoeuvring room and the ability to go it alone."[401] In a democracy, an inherent contradiction exists between the needs of the monetary union and politicians' freedom to fight the electoral battles.

For example, supporting policies that increase wage flexibility and labor mobility or cut government services doesn't win many votes. However, plenty of votes can be gained from pushing subsidies to targeted interest groups, protection of corporate income, and public investments that benefit specific regions. The benefits politicians accrue through such actions far outweigh their cost to society. Add in the voters' increasingly negative attitude toward monetary union, and the future begins to look bleak for the single currency.[402]

It seems fair to conclude that the hurdles the EMU faces on the road to becoming an optimum currency area are formidable. The crisis in the eurozone has only raised those hurdles. For example, when Merkel and Sarkozy came up with their pact for competitiveness in February 2011, the other member states' nationalistic reflexes killed the project on the spot.[403] The March 2011 and July 2011 European summits produced several initiatives that, in principle, should lead to greater political and fiscal union, more budgetary discipline, more structural reforms, better-functioning markets, and greater labor mobility. However, pushing those changes through will be a Herculean task.

Further complicating the situation, the policymaking environment has become restless, if not hostile. European policymakers lost substantial credibility as a result of messy policies and poor communication in their attempts to alleviate the crisis. Other factors contribute to this loss of credibility. Angel Ubide, director of global economics at Tudor Investment Corporation, notes that "with high debt levels and an adverse demographic outlook, debt intolerance has likely increased on a permanent basis."[404] Also, European leaders like Van Rompuy and Barroso are sidelined by the Merkels and the Sarkozys of the larger euro member states each time tough decisions need to be made, which does not improve trust in or the credibility of the European institutions.

For the time being, European policymakers will likely continue to muddle through (which I labeled as the MOS approach). Grandiloquent speeches and declarations will be followed by highly complex agreements and compromises that different leaders will each interpret differently, leading to renegotiation and starting the whole process over. More debt and credit will be added to the existing piles of debt and credit. The monetary union will become increasingly dependent on Germany, the country with the strongest economy and the deepest pockets. The danger that a Big Bang in German attitudes will fatally threaten the idea of a unified Europe has increased substantially with the crisis of the eurozone.

Dominant and Disliked

Barroso declared in May 2010, "Our community needs Germany in a leading role. Otherwise, we have a problem."[405] Since then, the eurozone has experienced what Ulrike Guérot and Mark Leonard of the European Council on Foreign Relations have described as "a 'unipolar moment' within the eurozone: no solution to the crisis was possible without Germany or against Germany."[406] According to the *Financial Times*, EC officials joke that the first question asked about any legislation is "What is Berlin's position on this?"[407] As German power and dominance grew, many of the country's partners found the behavior of Merkel's government often high-handed, inflexible, dogmatic, arrogant, and lacking solidarity with Germany's distressed European brethren.

With Germany both dominant and disliked in Europe, many wonder whether the country will withdraw from the eurozone. Many of Merkel's public statements suggest that such a move is out of the question. In one of her livelier and more spirited speeches, Merkel declared, "The euro is more than just a currency. It is our good fortune that we Europeans are united. A united Europe is the guarantor for our peace and our freedom. The euro is the basis of our economic well-being. Germany needs Europe and our common currency, for our own good, and for coping with global challenges."[408]

Merkel repeated this message on several occasions and joined the chorus of European politicians declaring that the euro will be saved "whatever it takes." On other occasions, however, she showed more reserve. "Yes, Germany will help. But Germany only helps when the others exert themselves as well…. You cannot have a common currency and, at the same time, have radically different social security systems."[409] At the end of 2010, the *Financial Times'* Gideon Rachman commented on the difficulty of predicting how the euro crisis will end:

> My current best guess is that single currency will indeed eventually break up—and that the euro's executioner will be Germany…. The Germans would not take this step lightly or quickly…but if the Germans became convinced that their eurozone partners were simply impossible to deal with—and that therefore the whole single currency experiment could not work—they might decide to quit.[410]

A few days later, Rachman's colleague Martin Wolf was more explicit: "The only ways out [of the mess several euro members are tumbling into] would be for the ECB to buy public debt or a fiscal union, with the capacity to bail out members in difficulty. Both are inconceivable. Germany would surely exit first."[411] Citigroup economists Willem Buiter and Ebrahim Rahbari add a timeframe to the discussion, arguing that "the changing of the generations in Germany from Kohl to Schröder and then to Merkel has weakened the traditional umbilical link of Germany, and especially Germany's political class, to the EU and the eurozone, but not [yet] to the point that one can reasonably envisage Germany leaving the eurozone and the EU. Given *half a decade* of funding and subsidizing other countries with unsustainable fiscal positions and no capacity or willingness to correct these, that could change" (italics mine).[412]

What would make Germany decide to leave the euro behind and install a *neumark*? The simple answer is that Germany will exit when it becomes too costly to keep the monetary brotherhood together, that is, when the *perceived* costs outweigh the *perceived* benefits. At least three issues will figure prominently in the German cost/benefit analysis:

- Germany's stability culture
- the economic calculation
- the new political realities in Germany

Stability *über Alles*

In the eyes of most Germans, an economically stable environment means low inflation and financial stability. This view stems directly from the memories of the economic, social, and political tragedies that followed the hyperinflation of the 1920s. Even for younger generations of Germans, the memory of those disastrous times is remarkably vivid. Former Chancellor Gerhard Schröder made this crystal clear when he claimed that "if you try to fight German stability culture, you are bound to lose. It's better not to start that game."[413]

The stability culture has even become part of Germany's constitution since the constitutional court in Karlsruhe, in its 1993 ruling on the Maastricht Treaty, defined "the aim of stability as the benchmark of the monetary union" and further, that "in the case the stability of the community fails, a dissociation (of Germany) from that community" is warranted.[414] This ruling clearly indicates that leaving a destabilized (by German standards) European monetary union would present no legal problems for Germany.

Financial instability in member countries of the monetary union will inevitably undermine the stability of the eurozone's economic and financial environment. If large economies such as Spain or Italy follow Greece, Portugal, and Ireland's path, the other EMU members will look to Germany, the big brother with the deep pockets. Providing the funding to help these countries would weigh heavily on Germany's public finances and its credit rating. The public uproar would surely be impressive.

The alternative route is that the ECB directly finances distressed euro members. The deal ironed out May 8 and 9, 2010 was the first step taken in that direction. During the summer of 2011, the ECB reluctantly walked further down this path. For Germany, this option would be just as unacceptable as having to cough up the funds itself, as it would bring the ECB under direct control of the political authorities. This possibility is basically what made Bundesbank president Axel Weber walk away from the succession of Jean-Claude Trichet as president of the ECB.[415] Germans are still acutely aware that political abuse of the central bank destroyed democracy and paved the way for the rise of Adolf Hitler.

When the news was released early on the morning of May 10, 2010 that the ECB would start to buy paper issued by Greece, Ireland, and Portugal, Paris rejoiced. This had less to do with compassion for the smaller European countries than with national self-interest. With the precedent of financing the three smaller countries a *fait accompli*, rejection of any future French requests in the same direction would be impossible. It goes without saying that if France, the second largest economy of the eurozone, found it difficult to raise money on its own, the situation would definitely be past the point where the EMU construct held any attraction for Germany.

Although ECB president Jean-Claude Trichet exhausted himself explaining that this drastic policy change would not affect the ECB's independence, the change marked a clear victory for the French political elite. French politicians, even members of right-wing parties, still unite behind the view Minister of Finance Pierre Bérégovoy laid out in 1989: "No to technocracy. Yes to democracy! Central bankers have no right to be given superior authority."[416] Three years later, France's president, François Mitterrand, argued that "it is going to be politicians and not technocrats who will decide about economic policy and thus about the implementation of monetary policy." His right-wing successor, Jacques Chirac, stated in 1996 that monetary union in Europe needed "a political power [capable] of showing monetary power clearly the limits of its action."[417]

However, during the crisis in the eurozone, German pleas to respect financial and budgetary orthodoxy came to exhibit a double standard. On the one hand, Germany pushed the troubled eurozone countries to clean financial and budgetary house on Germany's terms. On the other hand, Germany opposed the tough rules most others wanted to use when performing the stress tests on the European banks. The German banking sector is not only heavily exposed to Greek, Irish, Portuguese, and Spanish risks, it is traditionally one of the most leveraged banking sectors in Europe. The regional Landesbanken are in many respects comparable to the *cajas* in Spain. Ulrike Guérot and Mark Leonard claim that "there are many in German society—from parliamentarians to bankers—who have conspired to keep the issue of the liquidity of the German banks off the political agenda."[418] To these liquidity problems, solvency problems can certainly be added.

Tony Barber of the *Financial Times* succinctly summarized Germany's questionable attitude toward its banking sector:

> The truth about the eurozone's crisis, rarely aired in public by German policymakers, is that the rescues of Greece, Ireland and Portugal are at heart rescues of European banks—especially in France and Germany. Germany's current account surpluses…were channelled through its banks and investors abroad in risky assets. Restructuring these countries' debts would involve losses for German banks, especially several Landesbanken, public sector lenders that are under the influence of regional big wigs. Such politicians are terrified of the electoral punishment awaiting them if it emerges that the banks require recapitalisation, to be funded by the taxpayers. Far better, in their view, to pretend that the problem does not exist and that the solution to the eurozone's problem lies in

years of austerity in southern Europe and Ireland. The irony is that, until Europe's banks are cleaned up, the German-devised solution for the eurozone amounts to little more than a recipe for never-ending financial support for the area's weakest states.[419]

The Economic Calculus

The second set of issues surrounding the German appreciation of the costs and benefits of the monetary union and the euro deal with market access and competitiveness. All members of a monetary union use a single currency. In economic terms, the EMU is a free-trade zone that is internally guaranteed free of devaluations or revaluations of national currencies. From the 1960s on, the German industrial corporations continuously faced competition from countries that regularly devaluated their currencies versus the German mark. Italy in particular made regular devaluations of the lira a cornerstone of its social and economic policies. To a lesser extent the same was true of France and, later, Spain. Employment in and the growth potential of the German corporate sector were under constant pressure from these devaluations.

It hardly needs to be stressed that if Germany were to leave the euro behind, the value of its new currency would go up substantially against whatever currency the other countries chose. German companies leaning heavily on export markets and those competing fiercely with imported goods and services would immediately find themselves where they had started before the creation of the monetary union. Before the euro the German corporate sector had to invest, push productivity, and innovate constantly to compete with companies in countries that regularly devaluated their currencies. The German elite, particularly the industrial elite, have always seen the removal of the devaluation threat as an important advantage. It is not surprising that the powerful industrial lobby was always firmly in favor of a unified currency for Europe.

There is, however, an important difference between the pre-euro situation and the current one. The eurozone countries are still the most important market for German exports, but the importance of markets like China, India, Turkey, and Russia is rising rapidly. German exports to China almost doubled between 2009 and 2011.[420] At the end of 2011 German exports to France roughly equaled those to China. Germany alone accounts for 43 percent of EU exports to China, and this share is rising. The more important the non-euro areas become for German exports, the less the export industries (and their trade unions) will resist an exit from the monetary union. As German economist Jens Bastian remarked: "In the corporate sector, shifting trade patterns may signal that Europe does not necessarily come first anymore for many German businesses."[421] Ulrike Guérot and Mark Leonard write that some within the Bundesbank claim that "Germany needs the BRICS more than the PIIGS."[422]

Given the German corporate sector's historically staunch support of a unified currency, it's noteworthy that some of its leading spokesmen have started to attack the euro project. The most striking example of the new attitude is the book *Save Our Money*, written by Hans-Olaf Henkel, the former head of the Federation of German Industries. Henkel argues that the present eurozone should split up into a hard-currency union led by the Germans and a French-led southern group that could devalue its currency to regain competitiveness.[423] Earlier generations of German politicians would surely have rejected Henkel's arguments, but as a sign of the changing times, German Economics Minister Rainer Brüderle delivered a friendly speech at the launching event for Henkel's book. And Henkel is not alone. Dieter Spethmann, former chairman of the steel conglomerate Thyssen, asked to end the euro in its present form and create a northern euro.[424] Several times, the association of small German companies and entrepreneurs has expressed its strong doubts about the consequences for the German economy of the management of the euro crisis.

Despite all the commotion since the end of 2009, a large majority of German managers, entrepreneurs, and investors still strongly favor monetary union and the euro. However, as the crisis within the eurozone deepened, voices of opposition arose from this corner of German society. Concern for financial and monetary stability ranks high on the list of priorities for corporate Germany. In the end, adherence to the stability culture may dominate the concerns about corporate sales, market shares, and competitiveness.

A New Political Reality

The more problems within the monetary union endanger financial and economic stability, the more likely Germany is to consider an exit from the eurozone, despite the short-term disadvantages to the corporate sector. What Ulrike Guérot and Mark Leonard describe as the "new German euroscepticism" is further pushing Germany away from the monetary union, as the shift in public opinion demonstrates: "Since unification euroscepticism has become more socially acceptable, if not chic."[425] This shift can only be properly understood in a historical context.

German guilt over the Nazi regime's crimes and the role the country played in the two world wars has often driven its postwar politics. This could be labeled the Schmidt Doctrine, after Helmut Schmidt, who was chancellor of West Germany from 1974 to 1982. Schmidt declared in 1978 that "we (West Germans) are vulnerable on two fronts and will remain so until well into the next century. We are vulnerable, first, because of Berlin and because of the open flank in the East, because of the division of our nation, symbolised by Berlin's insular position. And we are vulnerable, second, because of Auschwitz. The more successful we are in the fields of foreign, economic, social and defence policy, the longer it will take for Auschwitz to fade from the fore of collective consciousness."[426]

Almost ten years later, Schmidt's humble awareness of Germany's past made him an ardent supporter of monetary union: "Without a common currency, the D-mark would over time play the leading role and the German banks and insurance companies would accomplish market-dominating position well beyond our borders, producing irritation and envy among others—and with malign political consequences for us Germans."[427] Jacob Kirkegaard, research fellow at the Peterson Institute for International Economics in Washington, recently restated the consequences of the Schmidt Doctrine: "It is politically unthinkable that Germany would undermine 60 years of pro-European policies by leaving the eurozone and thereby destroy the entire European Union, which has anchored its identity and powered its post-war authority."[428]

Mitterrand's threat to isolate Germany internationally scared Helmut Kohl into sacrificing the D-mark for a smooth reunification. However, Kohl was the last German chancellor to have personally experienced World War II. As Robert Kimmitt, American ambassador to Germany in the early 1990s, remembered, "Europe's history of war played an important role in the reasons for the single currency.… I recall how Chancellor Kohl took me into his garden at the back of his house saying, with emotion in his voice, how the blood of French and German soldiers had been spilled on all the land around."[429]

But Merkel and the politicians of her generation have only secondhand knowledge of World War II. After the fall of the Berlin Wall in 1989 swept away the postwar division of Germany, the country's troubled past became less of an issue. In the words of Wolfgang Proissl, the Brussels correspondent of the *Financial Times Deutschland*, "Most of today's [German] political class was born in the 1950s and 1960s. Many of them are indifferent towards European integration, some express scepticism or even hostility in private. For today's political class, working through the EU is just one policy option among several, and no longer a goal in itself."[430]

Greece's reaction to the tough austerity program it was forced to accept in return for a bailout fueled Germany's euroskeptic attitude.[431] Greek Deputy Prime Minister Theodoros Pangalos said in public that the offspring of Nazis had no right to issue orders to Greeks. The Greek newspaper *Ethnos* wrote that the Germans were turning Greece into a financial Dachau. The mayor of Athens went so far as to draw up an 80-billion-euro invoice for Wehrmacht's occupation of Greece during World War II.

Stronger but also Weaker

In July 2010, the German weekly *Die Zeit* asked, "Has the political DNA of Germany changed?"[432] Increasingly, the answer seems to be yes. Thomas de Mazière, one of Germany's top politicians, agreed, arguing,

> After 1990, Germany underwent a fundamental change. Until 1990, Germany was a divided country. It was economically strong but politically weak, and not really a fully sovereign state.... After 1990, not only the map of Germany but the map of Europe changed dramatically.... It may be new for Europe that Germany is representing its interests with new vigour. But for Britain, France or Italy, it was always a matter of course. We are also using new language in putting our arguments. We have to get used to this. The biggest net payer into the EU budget has to defend its interests.[433]

I do not mean to imply that the present generation of German politicians is in any way unaware of the country's past. My point is that they seem much less inclined to let that past dominate Germany's policies. In the words of Katinka Barysch, deputy director of the Centre for European Reform, "Today, many Germans think they have paid their historical dues."[434] In the second decade of the twenty-first century, Mitterrand's 1988 argument that "the

Germans are a great people deprived of certain attributes of sovereignty, with reduced diplomatic status"[435] is no longer valid.

More specifically, Germany's feelings of guilt no longer warrant paying a high price for European unity. As *The Economist* noted in early May 2010, "Germany has changed. The days of France having all the ideas and Germany paying all the bills are over."[436] The emerging German political class looks other countries straight in the eyes while forcefully defending German interest. Wolfgang Proissl argues convincingly that it can no longer be taken for granted that Germany will act as "Europe's benevolent hegemon."[437] As early as January 1990, Mitterrand had observed a distinct change in the German political mood. He explained to his counterpart in Britain, Margaret Thatcher, that "the problem of reunification has provoked a psychological shock with the Germans. This has revived certain characteristics that one had forgotten, a certain brutality and an elimination of all other problems apart from those corresponding to their own preoccupations."[438]

This evolution of the German political mindset has led to statements like former German Chancellor Gerhard Schröder's April 2007 argument that

> if France's political aim was to create the euro as part
> of a plan to weaken Germany so as to reduce our sup-
> posed economic dominance, then the result has been
> exactly the opposite. The rise in German competitive-
> ness means that Germany is stronger, not weaker. In a
> way, that is obvious and inevitable because we are the
> strongest economy in Europe.[439]

While the evidence certainly corroborates Schröder's claims, Germany's return to economic power and the country's new political assertiveness coincide with what Ulrike Guérot and Mark Leonard describe as Germany feeling

> more fragile from the inside. The old Federal Republic…
> had a consensus-driven political system, with strong trade
> unions, a relatively even distribution of national wealth,
> a functioning social elevator, good public schools, and
> a public health system that was accessible to all. Today's
> Germany, on the other hand, is older and poorer and
> faces more social problems than it used to. It is anxious
> about immigration, lags behind many OECD countries
> in terms of issues such as gender equality and child day
> care, and has an education system with huge flaws.[440]

Guérot and Leonard continue by arguing that Germany's now
much more fragmented political system makes

> political leadership—particularly that of the paternal-
> istic, pro-European variety—much harder. Whereas
> in the past German chancellors could override public
> opinion on critical foreign policy questions—as Konrad
> Adenauer did on rearmament in 1955, Willy Brandt
> did on Ostpolitik in 1972, and Kohl did on the station-
> ing of U.S. missiles in Germany in 1983 and again on
> the euro in 1992—today's leaders face a much more fis-
> siparous and complex political landscape.[441]

"Within the highest ranks of the German government," Wolfgang Proissl claims, "a talented charismatic populist might score
well on an anti-euro or pro-deutschmark platform."[442] Such considerations further increase the German political elite's receptiveness
to the idea of withdrawing from the European monetary union.

France in Decline

The changing German worldview must be considered in a broader
European context and especially in light of the relationship between Germany and France.[443] With rare exceptions, the partnership of these two countries since World War II has been strained.
The increased self-assurance of the Germans has heightened this

tension. Romano Prodi, the former president of the European Commission, described the change in the relationship: "It used to be said that France was the political driver and Germany the economic one.... Now it is the lady [Merkel] that decides and Sarkozy that holds a press conference to explain her decisions."[444]

France's inability to gracefully accept its political and economic decline has produced additional tension. *Le grandeur de la France*, once an undeniable reality, is now a thing of the past. Nevertheless, when China's largest bank, the Industrial & Commercial Bank of China (ICBC), opened an office in Paris, French Minister of Finance Christine Lagarde claimed that this move showed that China recognized "France as the financial market center of the Continent."[445] For France, accepting its reduced relevance meant giving up, in the words of leading French economist Jean-Hervé Lorenzi, "an iron rule respected since many centuries, being that of evoking France only as a great power."[446]

As we have argued, the French have consistently tried to use monetary union to control the Germans. The following comment, uttered by François Mitterrand in January 1990, is typical of the French elite: "I say that the Germans have the right to self-determination, but I say also that I have the right to take into account the preoccupations of the rest of Europe."[447] What Mitterrand meant by "the rest of Europe" is not so hard to guess.

France's loss of power and influence is plain to see. Paris is still a great metropolis to visit, with fabulous museums, a unique cultural and architectural heritage, and unsurpassed dining (and the French countryside remains genuinely beautiful). But it is no longer, as too many Frenchmen still assume (and, somewhat more rarely, brag about openly), the epicenter of the world. It is no longer even one of the leading capitals. As the twenty-first century advances, the United States and China are the only viable contenders for the top position, distantly followed by India, Japan, Brazil, Russia, and Germany. France's place is in the third tier, with Indonesia,

Turkey, Mexico, Iran, Saudi Arabia, South Korea, and the United Kingdom. The influence of these countries in major international discussions and initiatives is rarely decisive.

The inability to adjust to their reduced relevance makes French political leaders unpredictable. They know that an open admission of their reduced relevance would be a political disaster. So they twist and turn and try to outperform each other in trying to keep the reality about France more or less hidden. Hence, President Sarkozy's truly idiotic threat to withdraw from the EMU in May 2010, or the furious frustration of Sarkozy's predecessor, Jacques Chirac, when he tried to bully several Eastern European countries into an anti-American stance in the run-up to the American invasion of Iraq.

Despite its reduced relevance worldwide, France is still the second most important country in the eurozone. Moreover, the political and economic elite of France have no doubt as to the direction the European idea needs to take. Jean-Hervé Lorenzi writes that the French elite see "Europe as an extension of France" and describes "on old dream" of the French "to multiply in an almost mechanical way the economic, diplomatic and cultural capacities [of France] by the miracle of a unified Europe so as to come to a transposition of France on a European scale."[448] As that "old dream" moves further out of reach, French uneasiness with the European project rises commensurately with Germany's dominance. When Germany's officials do the political math on whether or not to stay in the European monetary union, the French factor will be high on their list of considerations.

Falling Out of Love
Germany, as Wolfgang Proissl put it, is

> falling out of love with Europe. That process started with
> reunification, which made the country less affluent and
> more inclined to affirm its national interests in the EU.

Then EMU laid the popular basis for euro-scepticism. Abandoning the deutschmark in favour of the euro was never accepted by many Germans. In recent years, the two governments of Chancellor Merkel stopped making the case for the country's engagement in Europe because it was felt that the EU was viewed negatively by voters and the less talk about Brussels the better.[449]

The reaction to Jean-Claude Trichet's June 2011 proposal for an EU finance ministry was typical of the change in German attitude. Alexander Dobrindt, secretary general of the CSU, the Bavarian sister party of Merkel's CDU, rejected Trichet's proposal quickly and firmly. Dobrindt even went in the opposite direction, writing a memorandum that explicitly pleaded for the transfer of powers back to Germany from the EU. German newspapers reported that Dobrindt opposed Trichet's proposal on the grounds that it would "reduce democracy and threaten sovereignty."[450] Katinka Barysch commented,

> perhaps for the first time since the second World War, [the Germans] are allowing themselves to be defiant and proud. Their export-oriented, stability-obsessed economic model is not up for discussion. Their participation in the eurozone is becoming more conditional. Even the wisdom of the whole EU project is now sometimes questioned.... For the generation of Helmut Kohl, Europe was a matter of war and peace. For Merkel and most of her contemporaries, it is a question of costs and benefits.[451]

That seems to be the best Europe will get from Germany for the time being. And that is small reassurance for the future of the monetary union and the euro.

Epilogue

FACTS ARE STUBBORN THINGS AND WHATEVER MAY BE OUR WISHES...THEY
CANNOT ALTER THE STATE OF FACTS AND EVIDENCE.

—*John Adams, second president of the United States*[452]

STRONG DEFENDERS OF EUROPEAN MONETARY UNI-
fication—for example, former German Chancellor Helmut
Kohl and former European Commission president Jacques
Delors—never hesitated to hint that the success or failure of monetary union and the euro would make the difference between war and peace for Europe. In spring 2010, Merkel and Sarkozy echoed this sentiment.

The monetary union and its single currency are the most visible expression of the attempts at greater European integration inspired by a desire never to repeat the horrors of the two world wars that started on European soil. If sixty-five years of peace in Europe can be attributed to these efforts, the judgment on monetary union should by all means be positive. However, there is more to this equation.

While efforts at European integration have without question contributed to peace on the continent, at least three other factors are also at play. First, broader international cooperation and consultation, for example through the United Nations, has also bene-fited Europe. Second, the presence of American troops throughout Europe, and certainly in Germany, helped maintain the military status quo. Third, the sense during the Cold War of a common, nondemocratic enemy increased cooperation and cohesion among Western European countries.

And peace itself is but one consequence of European monetary union and the single currency. The economic benefits of belonging to a monetary union are real and numerous. However, there are also costs. EMU remains incomplete in the sense that it does not fulfill several of the conditions for a smoothly and efficiently func-tioning monetary union. History teaches us that, in particular, the lack of real political union is a major barrier to the durability of a monetary union and its single currency. Given the EMU's incom-pleteness, the crisis that erupted savagely in the fall of 2009 should not have been a surprise. This crisis demonstrated the massive costs that EMU membership could entail for its members.

The sovereign debt crisis within the eurozone brought pain-fully to the forefront the many shortcomings of the European monetary construction and its governance. European authorities showed what one observer defined as "serial incompetence" in fighting the crisis. After initial denial of the seriousness of the cri-sis, they attempted to cure the symptoms rather than the disease itself by throwing money at the problem and by putting the Euro-pean Central Bank in a difficult and dangerous situation.

More of the same (MOS) is the route Europe will probably take in the shorter run. This approach leaves the fundamental problems untouched. Greece, Portugal, and Ireland will soon have no choice but to leave the monetary union (follow the throwing-out-the-sys-tem [TOS] option). The perilous state of their public finances and their poor growth prospects have turned Spain, Italy, Belgium and even France into likely next victims of the euro crisis.

If the European authorities do not succeed in rebuilding the system (the ROS approach), the eurozone will unravel, probably in a highly chaotic way. Germany, the largest and best performing economy of the eurozone, will try to exit before monetary and financial stability goes completely down the drain. A fast-growing hostile attitude toward all things euro in Germany will weaken the resistance against a German exit.

"Is the euro to the early twenty-first century what the League of Nations was to the early twentieth: a fine idea that became a political orphan and was condemned to unravel?" American commentator Roger Cohen asked at the end of 2010.[453] I fear the answer is yes, unless a rephrasing of one of Winston Churchill's most famous dicta comes true. Churchill once claimed of the United States that you can always count on that country to do the right thing, but only after it exhausts all the other options. Will we be able to make a similar claim with respect to the eurozone authorities?

Despite the deep crisis, the European authorities have done hardly anything really substantial about the fundamentally important issues: rebuilding the European banking sector, restoring the long-term sustainability of public finances, improving the structural growth performance of their economies and, most important of all, rebuilding the institutional framework of the monetary union to make it more durable and efficient. They are quickly running out of time. As a matter of fact, it is probably already too late.

Acknowledgments

I HAVE BEEN WRITING AND REWRITING THIS BOOK, at least in my thoughts, for almost fifteen years now. From the mid-1990s on, I was very critical of the way in which the European authorities went about creating a monetary union. There was much too much politics involved, and not nearly enough attention paid to the economics—thus thwarting any attempts to build a sound monetary union. As editor in chief of the Belgian weekly *Trends,* I ventilated my doubts regularly. At best, these remarks were received with gentle smiles. Most of the time, politicians ridiculed the warnings. Today, it's not a good feeling to know that my early objections and critical remarks have been vindicated by reality.

Over the years, I had numerous discussions with countless people at central banks on the issues involved. I talked to decision makers and economists at the Federal Reserve Bank, the European Central Bank, the Nationale Bank van België, the Nederlandsche Bank, the Bundesbank, the Bank of England, the Banque de France, the Bank of Sweden, the International Monetary Fund, and the Bank for International Settlements. Most of those discussions were off the record. It's primarily for that reason that the discussions were often enormously informative and stimulating.

Although naming names is not an option here, I thank all of these people from the bottom of my heart for the insights and arguments they provided so eloquently.

Special thanks go to my former professors Emiel Van Broekhoven and Walter Nonneman, who are both great economists and superb human beings. The same holds for Geert Noels, the founder, CEO, and chief economist of Econopolis. Geert remains beyond any doubt the very best biker-economist on the planet. Several of my colleagues at *Trends* contributed to the book. Other Belgian economists who regularly offered inspiring comments are Joep Konings, Erik Buyst, Luc Sels, Filip Abraham, Herman Daems, Jef Vuchelen, Geert Janssens, Peter De Keyzer, and Ivan Van De Cloot. I also benefitted from occasional and often more structured discussions with, among many others, Anil Kashyap, Bob Aliber, Luigi Zingales and Randall Kroszner (The University of Chicago Booth School of Business), Edmund Phelps (Columbia University), Robert Barro (Harvard), Harold James (Princeton), Douglas Urwin (Dartmouth College), and Daron Acemoglu (MIT).

Obviously, I also thank my family for their support during the creation of this book.

Bibliography

Aeschimann, E., and P. Riché. 1996, *La Guerre de Sept Ans: Histoire Secrete du Franc Fort, 1989-1996*. Paris: Calman-Lévy.

Alesina, A., and F. Giavazzi, eds. 2010, *Europe and the Euro*. Chicago: University of Chicago Press.

Alesina, A., and F. Giavazzi. 2006. *The Future of Europe: Reform or Decline*. Cambridge, MA: MIT Press.

Alesina, A., and R. Barro. 2002. "Currency Unions." *Quarterly Journal of Economics* 117 (2): 409–36.

Allen, P. R. 1976. "Organisation and Administration of a Monetary Union." Princeton, NJ: Princeton University Press.

Artis, M. 2002. "Reflections on Optimal Currency Area (OCA) Criteria in the Light of EMU." Working paper, Central Bank of Chile.

Artis, M., and W. Zhang. 2002. "Membership of EMU: A fuzzy Clustering Analysis of Alternative Criteria." *Journal of Economic Integration* 17 (1): 54–79.

Athanassiou, P. 2009. "Withdrawal and Expulsion from the EU and EMU: Some Reflections." Legal working paper, European Central Bank.

Attali, J. 2005. *C'était François Mitterrand*. Paris: Fayard.

Baldwin, R., D. Gros, and L. Laeven. 2010. *Completing the Eurozone Rescue: What More Needs to Be Done?* Accessed 7/24/11. www.voxeu.org/index.php?q=node/5194.

Barysch, K. 2010. *Germany, the Euro and the Politics of the Bail-Out*. London: Centre for European Reform.

Bertola, G. 2000. "Labor Markets in the European Union." Brussels, Belgium: European Commission.

Bini Smaghi, Lorenzo. 2011a. "Eurozone, European Crisis, and Policy Responses." Speech at the Goldman Sachs Global Macro Conference, Hong Kong, February 22.

———. 2011b. "Private Sector Involvement: From (Good) Theory to (Bad) Practice." Speech at the Reinventing Bretton Woods Committee, Berlin, Germany, June 6.

Blair, T. 2010. *A Journey: My Political Life*. New York: Alfred A. Knopf.

Bootle, R. 2009. *The Trouble with Markets: Saving Capitalism from Itself*. London: Nicholas Brealey Publishing.

Bordo, M. 2004. "The United States as a Monetary Union and the Euro: A Historical Perspective." *Cato Journal* 24 (1–2).

Bordo, M., and L. Jonung. 1999. "The Future of EMU: What Does History of Monetary Unions Tell Us?" Working paper, NBER.

———. 2000. *Lessons For EMU from the History of Monetary Unions*. London: Institute of Economic Affairs.

Brown, G. 2010. *Beyond the Crash: Overcoming the First Crisis of Globalization*. New York: Free Press.

Buiter, W. 1999. "Alice in Euroland." *Journal of Common Market Studies* 37 (2): 181–209.

Buiter, W., G. Corsetti, and N. Roubini. 1992. "Excessive Deficits: Sense and Nonsense in the Treaty of Maastricht." *Economic Policy* 8 (16).

Buiter, W., and E. Rahbari. 2010. "Greece and the Fiscal Crisis in the Eurozone." Centre for Economic Policy Research Policy Insight no. 51.

Buiter, W., E. Rahbari, J. Michels, and G. Giani, 2011. "The Debt of Nations." Global Economics View, Citigroup Global Markets, January 7.

Buiter, W., and A. Sibert. 2006. "How the Eurosystem's Open-Market Operations Weaken Financial Market Discipline (And What to Do About It)." Working paper, Centre for Economic Policy Research.

Buti, M., S. Deroose, V. Gaspar, and J. Nogueira Martins. 2010. *The Euro: The First Decade*. Cambridge, UK: Cambridge University Press.

Calvo, G., and C. Reinhart. 2000. "The Fear of Floating." College Park, MD: University of Maryland.

Carmassi, J., and S. Micosi. 2010. "The Role of Politicians in Inciting Financial Markets to Attack the Eurzone." Centre for European Policy Studies Commentary no. 4.

Chivvis, C. 2010. *The Monetary Conservative: Jacques Rueff and Twentieth-Century Free Market Thought*. DeKalb, IL: Northern Illinois University Press.

Committee for the Study of Economic and Monetary Union. 1989. "Report on Economic and Monetary Union in the European Community." Brussels, Belgium: Committee for the Study of Economic and Monetary Union.

Connolly, B. 1995. *The Rotten Heart of Europe: The Dirty War for Europe's Money*. London: Faber and Faber.

Coombes, D. 1970. *Politics and Bureaucracy in the European Community: A Portrait of the Commission of the E.E.C.* London: Allen & Unwin.

Corden, W. M. 1972. *Monetary Integration: Essays in International Finance*. Princeton, NJ: Princeton University Press.

———. 2002. *Too Sensational: On the Choice of Exchange Rate Regimes*. Cambridge, MA: MIT Press.

Cottarelli, C., L. Forni, J. Gottschalk, and P. Mauro. 2010, "Default in Today's Advanced Economies: Unnecessary, Undesirable and Unlikely." Washington, DC: International Monetary Fund.

Dadush, U., ed. 2010. *Paradigm Lost: The Euro in Crisis*. Washington, DC: Carnegie Endowment for International Peace.

Davies, H., and D. Green. 2010. *Banking on the Future: The Fall and Rise of Central Banking*. Princeton, NJ: Princeton University Press.

De Bandt, O., and F. P. Mongelli. 2000. "Convergence of Fiscal Policies in the Euro Area." Working Paper, European Central Bank.

De Cecco, M., and A. Giovanni, eds. 1989. *A European Central Bank? Perspectives on Monetary Unification After Ten Years of the EMS*. Cambridge, UK: Cambridge University Press.

De Grauwe, P. 1994. "Monetary Policies in the EMS: Lessons from the Great Recession of 1991–93." Centre for Economic Policy Research Discussion paper no. 1047.

———. 2003. *Economics of Monetary Union*, 5th edition. Oxford, UK. Oxford University Press.

De Grauwe, P., and F. Mongelli. 2005. "Endogeneities of Optimum Currency Areas: What Brings Countries Sharing a Single Currency Closer Together?" Working paper, European Central Bank.

Duval, R., and J. Elmeskov. 2006. "The Effects of EMU on Structural Reforms in Labour and Product Markets." Working paper, Organisation for Economic Co-operation and Development.

Dyson, K., ed. 2008. *The Euro at Ten: Europeanization, Power, and Convergence*. Oxford, UK: Oxford University Press.

Eichengreen, B. 2011. *Exorbitant Privilege: The Rise and Fall of the Dollar and the Future of the International Monetary System*. Oxford, UK: Oxford University Press.

———. 2009. "Was the Euro a Mistake?" Accessed 7/24/11. http://voxeu.org/index.php?q=node/2815.

———. 2007. "The Euro: Love It or Leave It?" Accessed 7/24/11. www.voxeu.org/index.php?q=node/729.

———. 1997. *European Monetary Unification: Theory, Practice, and Analysis*. Cambridge, MA: MIT Press.

———. 1993. "European Monetary Unification." Journal of Economic Literature 31 (3): 1321–57.

———.1992. "Should the Maastricht Treaty Be Saved?" Princeton Studies in International Finance no. 74. Princeton, NJ: Princeton University Press.

Eichengreen, B., and J. Frieden, eds. 2000. *The Political Economy of European Monetary Unification*. Boulder, CO: Westview.

Eichengreen, B., and C. Wyplosz. 1997. "The Stability Pact: Minor Nuisance, Major Diversion?" *Economic Policy* 26: 65–114.

Emerson, M., D. Gros, A. Italianer, J. Pisani-Ferry, and H. Reichenbach. 1992. *One Market, One Money: An Evaluation of the Potential Benefits and Costs of Forming an Economic and Monetary Union*. Oxford: Oxford University Press.

Emminger, O. 1977. "The D-Mark in the Conflict Between Internal and External Equilibrium 1948–1975." *Essays in International Finance* no. 122. Princeton, NJ: Princeton University Press.

———. 1986. *D-Mark, Dollar, Währungskrisen: Erinnerungen eines ehemaligen Bundesbankpräsidenten*. Stuttgart, Germany: Deutsche Verlags-Anstalt.

European Commission. 2008. "EMU@10: Successes and Challenges of Ten Years of EMU." Brussels, Belgium: European Commission.

———. 2002. "Free Movement of Workers: Achieving the Full Benefits and Potential." Brussels, Belgium: European Commission.

Feldstein, M. 2000. "The European Central Bank and the Euro: The First Year." Working paper, NBER.

———. 1999. "The Euro Risk." *Time Magazine Europe*, January 25.

———. 1997. "EMU and International Conflict." *Foreign Affairs* 76 (6).

———. 1992. "The Case Against EMU." *Time Magazine*, June 13.

Ferguson, N. 2001. *The Cash Nexus: Money and Power in the Modern World, 1700–2000*. New York: Basic Books.

Fleming, M. 1971. "On Exchange Rate Unification." *Economic Journal* 13 (26): 467–88.

Frankel, J., and A. Rose. 1997. "Is EMU More Justifiable Ex Post than Ex Ante?" *European Economic Review* 41 (3): 753–60.

———. 1996. "The Endogeneity of the Optimum Currency Area Criteria." Working paper, NBER.

Friedman, M. 1950. "The Case for Flexible Exchange Rates." In *Essays in Positive Economics*, edited by M. Friedman. Chicago: University of Chicago Press.

Friedman, M., and A. Schwartz. 1963. *A Monetary History of the United States*. Princeton, NJ: Princeton University Press.

Genscher, H. 1995. *Erinnerungen*. Berlin, Germany: Siedler.

Giavazzi, F., and A. Giovannini. 1989. *Limiting Exchange Rate Flexibility: The European Monetary System*. Cambridge, MA: MIT Press.

Gokhale, J. 2009. "Measuring the Unfunded Obligations of European Countries." Cato Insitute Policy Report no. 319.

Goldman Sachs. 2008. *The Euro at Ten: Performance and Challenges for the Next Decade*. Goldman Sachs.

Goldstein, M., and N. Véron. 2011. "Too Big to Fail: The Transatlantic Debate." Working paper, Bruegel.

Grant, C. 1994. *Delors: Inside the House that Jacques Built*. London: Nicholas Brealey Publishing.

Greenlaw, D., S. S. Hyun, A. Kashyap, and K. Schoenholtz. 2011. "Stressed Out: Macroprudential Principles for Stress Testing." U.S. Monetary Policy Forum Report no. 5, Initiative on Global Markets, University of Chicago Booth School of Business.

Gros, D., and N. Thygesen. 1992. *European Monetary Integration: From the European Monetary System Towards Monetary Union*. London: Longman.

Guérot, U., and M. Leonard. 2011. "The New German Question: How Europe Can Get the Germany It Needs." European Council on Foreign Relations Policy Brief no. 30.

Guigou, E. 2000. *Une Femme au Coeur de l'Etat*. Paris: Fayard.

Haberler, G. 1970. "The International Monetary System: Some Recent Developments and Discussions." In *Approaches to Greater Flexibility in Exchange Rates*, edited by G. Halm. Princeton, NJ: Princeton University Press.

Haufler, A., B. Lucke, M. Merz, and W. Richter. 2011. "The Plenum of German Economists on the European Debt Crisis." Accessed 7/24/11. http://voxeu.org/index.php?q=node/6153.

Henkel, H. 2010. *Rettet unser Geld! Deutschland wird ausverkauft—wie der Euro-Betrug unserem Wohlstand gefährdet*. Munich, Germany: Heyne.

Hoffmann, S. 1995. *The European Sisyphus: Essays on Europe, 1964–1994*. Boulder, CO: Westview Press.

Ingram, J. 1973. *The Case for European Monetary Integration: Essays in International Finance*. Princeton, NJ: Princeton University.

———. 1962. *Regional Payments Mechanisms. The Case of Puerto Rico*. Chapel Hill, NC: University of North Carolina Press.

International Monetary Fund (IMF). 1993. "Prologue to the ERM Crisis: Convergence Play." International Capital Markets.

Ip, G. 2010. *The Little Book of Economics: How the Economy Works in the Real World.* Hoboken, NJ: John Wiley & Sons.

Issing, O. 2011. *Moment of Truth Postponed.* London: Office of Monetary and Financial Institutions Forum.

———. 2002. *Should We Have Faith in Central Banks?* London: Institute of Economic Affairs.

Jacobi, L., and J. Kluve. 2006. "Before and After the Hartz Reforms: The Performance of Active Labor Market Policy in Germany." Rhine-Westphalia Institute for Economic Research Discussion paper no. 41.

James, H. 1996. *International Monetary Cooperation Since Bretton Woods.* New York: Oxford University Press.

Jenkins, R. 1991. *A Life at the Centre.* London: Macmillan.

Jonsson, A. 2009. *Why Iceland?* New York: McGraw Hill.

Jonung, L. 2010. "Greece and the Crisis in the Euro." Lecture at the 11th Trento Summer School.

Jonung, L. and E. Drea. 2009. "The Euro: It Can't Happen. It's a Bad Idea. It Won't Last. U.S. Economists on the EMU, 1989–2002." European Commission Economic paper no. 395.

Kenen, P. 1969. "The Theory of Optimum Currency Areas: An Eclectic View." In *Monetary Problems of the International Economy*, edited by R. Mundell and A. Swoboda. Chicago: University of Chicago Press.

Kim, S. 1998. "Economic Integration and Convergence." *Journal of Economic History* 29 (1): 1–32.

Kirkegaard, J. 2010. "In Defense of Europe's Grand Bargain." Washington, DC: Peterson Institute for International Economics.

Kissinger, H. 1994. *Diplomacy.* New York: Simon & Schuster.

Kohl, H. 2005. Memoirs. London, Weidenfeld and Nicolson.

Kok Group. 2004. "Facing the Challenge: The Lisbon Strategy for Growth and Employment." Report from the High Level Group, Luxembourg.

Krugman, P. 2011. "Can Europe Be Saved?" *New York Times Magazine*, January 12.

Krugman, P., and A. Venables. 1996. "Integration, Specialization, and Adjustment." *European Economic Review* 40 (3): 959–67.

Lachman, D. 2011. *Can the Euro Survive?* London: Legatum Institute.

Lannoo, K. 2010. "The Bank Stress Tests: A Work in Progress." Brussels, Begium: Centre for European Policy Studies.

Lawson, N. 1992. *The Vision from No. 11: Memoirs of a Tory Radical.* London: Bantam Books.

Lester, R. 1939. *Monetary Experiments: Early American and Recent Scandinavian*. New York: August M. Kelley.

Lorenzi, J. 2011. *Le Fabuleux Destin d'une Puissance Intermédiaire*. Paris: Editions Grasset & Fasquelle.

Lynn, M. 2011. *Bust: Greece, the Euro, and the Sovereign Debt Crisis*. Hoboken, NJ: Bloomberg Press.

Margo, R. A. 1998. "Labor Market Integration Before the Civil War." Working paper, NBER.

Marjolin Study Group. 1975. *On Economic and Monetary Union 1980*. Brussels, Belgium: Commission of the EEC.

Marsh, D. 2009. *The Euro: The Politics of the New Global Currency*. New Haven, CT: Yale University Press.

———. 1994. *Germany and Europe: The Case of Unity*. London: Heinemann.

———. 1992. *The Bundesbank: The Bank that Rules Europe*. London: Heinemann.

Marshall, M. 1999. *The Bank: The Birth of Europe's Central Bank and the Rebirth of Europe's Power*. London: Random House.

Mauldin, J., and J. Tepper. 2011. *Endgame: The End of the Debt Supercycle and How It Changed Everything*. Hoboken, NJ: John Wiley & Sons.

McCusker, J. 1978. *Money and Exchange in Europe and America, 1600–1775: A Handbook*. Chapel Hill, NC: University of North Carolina Press.

McKinnon, R. 1963. "Optimum Currency Areas." *American Economic Review* 53 (4): 717–25.

Mélitz, J. 1996. "The Theory of Optimum Currency Areas, Trade and Adjustment." *Open Economies Review* 7 (2): 99–116.

Milward, A., 1984. *The Reconstruction of Western Europe, 1945–51*. Berkeley, CA: University of California Press.

Mintz, N. N. 1970. "Monetary Union and Economic Integration." *The Bulletin*, New York University.

Mitterrand, F. 1996. *De l'Allemagne, de la France*. Paris: Editions Odile Jacob.

Molloy, R., C.L. Smith and A. Wozniak. 2011, "Internal Migration in the United States." Finance and Economics Discussion Series, Federal Reserve Board, Washington, 2011-30.

Mongelli, F. P. 2002. "'New' Views on the Optimum Currency Area Theory: What is EMU Telling Us?" Working paper, European Central Bank.

Mundell, R. 1973. "Uncommon Arguments for Common Currencies." In *The Economics of Common Currencies*, edited by H. Johnson and A. Svoboda. London: Allen & Unwin.

———. 1961. "A Theory of Optimum Currency Areas." American Economic Review 51 (3): 657–65.

Nechio, F. 2010. "The Greek Crisis: Argentina Revisited?" Federal Reserve Bank of San Francisco Economic Letter no. 33.

Nielsen, A. 1937. "Monetary Unions." In Encyclopedia of the Social Sciences. New York: Macmillan Company.

Nolling, W. 1993. Unser Geld: Der Kampf um die Stabilität der Wahrungen in Europa. Berlin, Germany: Ulstein.

Obstfeld, M. 1997. "Europe's Gamble." Brookings Papers on Economic Activity, Washington no. 2.

Obstfeld, M., J. Shambaugh, and A. Taylor. 2005. "The Trilemma in History: Trade-offs Among Exchange Rates, Monetary Policy, and Capital Mobility." Review of Economics and Statistics 87 (3): 423–38.

Organisation for Economic Co-operation and Development (OECD). 2000. EMU One Year On. Paris: OECD.

———. 1999. EMU: Facts, Challenges and Policies. Paris: OECD.

Padoa-Schioppa, T. 2000. The European Union and the Nation State. Hume Occasional Paper no. 58.

Proissl, W. 2010. "Why Germany Fell Out of Love with Europe." Bruegel Essay and Lecture Series (forthcoming).

Prior-Wandesforde, R., and G. Hacche. 2005. "European Meltdown? Europe Fiddles as Rome Burns." London: HSBC.

Reinhart, C., and K. Rogoff. 2009. This Time Is Different: Eight Centuries of Financial Folly. Princeton, NJ: Princeton University Press.

Reis, J., ed. 1995. International Monetary Systems in Historical Perspective. London: Macmillan.

Robson, P. 1987. The Economics of International Integration. London: Allen & Unwin.

Rockoff, H. 2003. "How Long Did It Take the United States to Become an Optimal Currency Area?" In Monetary Unions: Theory, History, Public Choice, edited by F. H. Capie and G. E. Wood. London: Routledge.

Rodden, J. 2006. Hamilton's Paradox: The Promise and Peril of Fiscal Federalism. Cambridge, UK: Cambridge University Press.

Sala-i-Martin, X., and J. Sachs. 1992. "Federal Fiscal Policy and Optimum Currency Areas." In Establishing a Central Bank: Issues in Europe and Lessons from U.S., edited by M. Canzoneri, V. Grilli, and P. Masson. Cambridge, UK: Cambridge University Press.

Samuelson, P., and W. Barnett, eds. 2007. *Inside the Economist's Mind: Conversations with Eminent Economists*. Oxford, UK: Blackwell Publishing.

Schlesinger, H. 1996. "Money Is Just the Start." *The Economist*, September 21.

Sinn, H.W. 1996. "International Implications of German Unification." Working paper, National Bureau of Economic Research.

Smigiel, J. 2010. "Free Movement of Workers in the European Union: Obstacles to EU Labor Mobility and Possibilities to Overcome Them." MA dissertation, Central European University.

Solow, R. 2002. "Is Fiscal Policy Possible? Is It Desirable?" Presidential Address to the XIII World Congress of the International Economic Association, Lisbon.

Steinberg, J. 2011. *Bismarck: A Life*. Oxford, UK: Oxford University Press.

Szasz, A.1999. *The Road to European Monetary Union*. London: Macmillan.

Tavlas, G. 1994. "The Theory of Monetary Integration." *Open Economies Review* 5(2): 211–30.

———. 1993. "The 'New' Theory of Optimum Currency Areas." *World Economy* 16(6): 663–85.

Thatcher, M. 2002. *Statecraft. Strategies for a Changing World*. New York: Harper Collins.

Theurl, T. 1992. *Eine gemeinsame Währung für Europa, 12 Lehren aus der Geschichte*. Innsbruck, Austria: Osterreichischer Studien Verlag

Tilford, S. 2011. "Debt Restructuring Will Not End the Euro Crisis." Centre for European Policy Reform CER blogspot, May 10.

———. 2010a. "Closing the Gap Between Rhetoric and Reality Is Key to the Euro's Survival." Centre for European Policy Reform CER blogspot, May 10

———. 2010b. "The Euro's Reality Gap." *CER Bulletin* June/July, Issue 72.

———. 2009. "The Euro at Ten: Is Its Future Secure?" London: Centre for European Reform Essays.

———. 2006. "Will the Eurozone Crack?" London: Centre for European Reform.

Tilford, S., and P. Whyte. 2010. *The Lisbon Scorecard X: The Road to 2020*. London: Centre for European Reform.

Torres, F., and F. Giavazzi, eds. 1993. *Adjustments and Growth in the European Monetary Union*. Cambridge, UK: Cambridge University Press.

Trichet, J. 2011a. "Competitiveness and the Smooth Functioning of EMU." Lecture at the University of Liège, Liège, Belgium, February 23.

———. 2011b. "Building Europe, Building Institutions." Speech on receiving the Karlspreis 2011, Aachen, Germany, June 2.

————. 1992. "Dix Ans de Disinflation Competitive." *Les Notes Bleues de Bercy*, 1–12.

Van Bergeijk, P., R. Berndsen, and J. Jansen, eds. 2000. *The Economics of the Euro Area: Macroeconomic Policy and Institutions*. Cheltenham, UK: Edward Elgar.

Van Overtveldt, J. 2010. *Bernanke's Test: Ben Bernanke, Alan Greenspan, and the Drama of the Central Banker*. Chicago, Agate.

————. 2003. *De Euroscheppers: Macht en Manipulatie Achter de Euro*. Kapellen, Belgium: Uitgeverij Pelckmans.

Vanthoor, W. 1996. *European Monetary Union since 1848: A Political and Historical Analysis*. Cheltenham, UK: Edward Elgar.

Weber, A. 2010. "Monetary Policy after the Crisis: A European Perspective." Keynote speech at the Shadow Open Market Committee (SOMC) symposium, New York, October 12.

Werner Plan. 1970. "Report to the Council and the Commission on the Realization by Stages of Economic and Monetary Union in the Community." Luxembourg: Bulletin of the European Communities, Supplement II.

Witteveen, H. J. 1970. "Munt slaan uit de Europese eenheid." Address to the Dutch Organization for the International Chamber of Commerce, Amsterdam, Netherlands, May 26.

Wyplosz, C. 2010. "The Failure of the Lisbon Strategy." Accessed 7/24/11. www.voxeu.org/index.php?q=node/4478.

————. 2006. "European Monetary Union: The Dark Sides of a Major Success." *Economic Policy* 46 (4): 207–61.

————. 2001. *The Impact of EMU on Europe and the Developing Countries*. Oxford, UK: Oxford University Press.

Endnotes

1. Schäuble as quoted in the *Financial Times*, December 6, 2010.
2. Lagarde as quoted in the *Financial Times*, December 4, 2010.
3. Proell as quoted by Associated Press, May 10, 2010
4. Borg as quoted in the *Financial Times*, May 17, 2010.
5. Tilford, 2010a, p. 2.
6. *Financial Times*, May 10, 2010.
7. Annunziata as quoted in the *Financial Times*, May 17, 2010.
8. Van Rompuy as quoted in the Dutch newspaper *NRC Handelsblad*, December 24, 2010.
9. Major as quoted in Marsh, 2009, p. 162.
10. Eichengreen, 2009, p. 1.
11. *Financial Times*, March 26, 2011.
12. Ferguson, 2001, p. 338.
13. Jonung and Drea, 2009.
14. Vanthoor, 1996, p. xiii.
15. Following Allen, 1976.
16. For more on this monetary union, see McCusker, 1978.
17. The classic reference on the monetary history of the United States remains Friedman and Schwartz, 1963.
18. Most of what follows on German monetary union is based on Holtfrerich, C., "The Monetary Unification Process in Nineteenth-Century Germany: Relevance and Lessons for Europe Today," in de Cecco and Giovanni, 1989.
19. See Theurl, 1992 and Vanthoor, 1996 for more on the Italian and Swiss experiences.
20. An attempt to enlarge the monetary union to Austria was started in 1857 but abandoned after a few years due to "the underlying serious political tensions between the participating countries." (Vanthoor, 1996, p. 31)
21. For more on the fascinating figure of Otto von Bismarck, also the inventor of modern social security systems, see Steinberg, 2011.
22. Bagehot as quoted in *The Economist*, April 9, 1998.
23. Flandreau, Marc, "Was the Latin Monetary Union a Franc Zone?" in Reis, J., ed., 1995.
24. Vanthoor, 1996, p. 32.
25. Ibid., p. 37.
26. Most of the discussion on SMU is based on Henriksen, Ingrid, and Kaergard, Niels, "The Scandinavian Currency Union, 1875-1914" in Reis, J, ed., 1995.
27. Lester, 1939.
28. Vanthoor, 1996, p. 133, 132.

29. Lusser in the article "Währungsunion erfordert viel Solidärität" that appeared in the German newspaper *Die Welt* December 5, 1992.
30. Bordo, 2004, p. 163.
31. Churchill as quoted in Vanthoor, 1996, p. 62. It is often forgotten that Churchill did not see the UK as a member of those United States of Europe. For Churchill, the issue was exclusively related to the continental countries.
32. Marsh, 2009, p. 32.
33. Named after its initiator, U.S. Secretary of State George Marshall.
34. Milward, 1984.
35. In 1960 the OEEC was transformed into the Organisation for Economic Co-operation and Development (OECD), which still exists today as an economic think tank and policy-advising institution for developed countries.
36. Adenauer as quoted in Kissinger, 1994, p. 547.
37. Rueff as quoted in Marshall, 1999, p. 159. For more on the intriguing figure of Jacques Rueff, see Chivvis, 2010. More than half a century later, Otmar Issing, the German member of the first Executive Board of the ECB and generally recognized as a major architect of the ECB's policies during the first years of its operations, rephrased Rueff's statement as follows: "Europe will be built on *stable* money or it will not be built." See Issing, 2002, p. 40.
38. The Spaak Report was so named after Paul-Henri Spaak, the Belgian foreign minister who chaired the committee.
39. Coombes, 1970, p. 54.
40. Marjolin as quoted in Szasz, 1999, p. 8.
41. The French under the leadership of Charles de Gaulle sharply attacked the so-called "exorbitant privilege" the Americans enjoyed with the Bretton–Woods System. The basic characteristic of this exorbitant privilege was that Americans could essentially print as many dollars as they wanted to finance their deficits. For an excellent update on the issue of the exorbitant privilege, see Eichengreen, 2011.
42. See Emminger, 1977 and 1986.
43. Marsh, 2009, p. 54.
44. Werner Plan, 1970.
45. Kohl as quoted in Guigou, 2000, p. 73.
46. Mitterrand as quoted in Marsh, 2009, p. 115.
47. Blessing as quoted in Marsh, 2009, p. 40.
48. In fact, there were only five different currencies, since Belgium and Luxembourg shared the same franc.
49. This image referred to the fact that the international agreements at that time foresaw fluctuation margins of 4.5 percent around the parities against the dollar. To make things even more complicated, there existed "a worm crawling within the snake in the tunnel": the Benelux countries limited the fluctuation margins between their currencies to 1.5 percent.
50. During the following quarter century the membership of the European Community (later the European Union) increased to twenty-seven. Greece joined in 1981; Spain and Portugal in 1986; Austria, Finland, and Sweden in 1995; Cyprus, the Czech Republic, Estonia, Hungary, Latvia, Lithuania, Malta, Poland, Slovakia, and Slovenia in 2004; and Bulgaria and Romania in 2007. There are still frequent references to the EU-15 group, which consists of the fifteen countries that had joined the EU by 1995.

51. Vanthoor, 1996, p. 81.
52. Marjolin Study Group, 1975, p. 6.
53. Marsh, 2009, p. 65.
54. Giscard as quoted in Marsh, 2009, p. 69.
55. See Emminger, 1977 and 1986.
56. See the contribution of Helmut Schmidt to the German weekly *Die Zeit,* August 6, 1993.
57. For more on van Ypersele, see Van Overtveldt, 2003, especially footnote 24 to Chapter 2.
58. Jenkins, 1991, p. 481.
59. Pöhl as quoted in Marsh, 1992, p. 233.
60. Padoa-Schioppa as quoted in Marsh, 2009, p. 11.
61. On this strategy, see Giavazzi and Giovannini, 1989.
62. Wyplosz, 2006, p. 210.
63. Genscher, 1995.
64. Committee for the Study of Economic and Monetary Union, 1989.
65. Wyplosz, 2006, p. 212.
66. For more perspective on the trilemma, see Obstfeld, Shambaugh, and Taylor, 2005.
67. The most powerful statement of the case for flexible exchange rates remains Friedman, 1950.
68. Marsh, 2009, p. 120.
69. Pöhl as quoted in Marsh, 2009, p. 123.
70. For more on this aspect of Mitterrand's personality, see for example Marsh, 2009, p. 103 and 107.
71. Sinn, 1996, p. 1.
72. Rocard as quoted in Marsh, 2009, p. 137.
73. Thatcher, 2002, p.2. See Mitterrand, 1996 for many references by the French president to the fact that he understood very well the strategic opportunities offered by the German unification process.
74. Marsh, 1994, p. 15.
75. Kohl, 2005, p. 937.
76. See on this episode Genscher, 1995, Guigou, 2000, and Attali, 2005.
77. Marsh, 2009, p. 137.
78. In December 1995, it was determined that the single currency would be called the *euro.*
79. Waigel as quoted in *EuropaInterview,* December 1991. All this does not mean, however, that there was no resistance in Germany to the Maastricht Treaty. As a matter of fact, Wilhelm Nölling, a former member of the Bundesbank Central Council, voiced sharp criticism. See Nölling, 1993.
80. Gros and Thygesen, 1992, p. 166.
81. For more on this, see De Grauwe, 1994, and Sinn, 1996.
82. IMF, 1993.
83. Ibid.
84. Trichet as quoted in Marsh, 2009, p. 150. This quote by Trichet outraged the leaders of several other countries, the Germans not least among them.
85. Rieke as quoted in Marsh, 2009, p. 150.

86. Marsh, 2009, p. 10.
87. Duisenberg as quoted in the *International Herald Tribune,* October 30, 2000.
88. Pöhl as quoted in Sinn, 1996, p. 22 (fn. 19).
89. Delors as quoted in Issing, 2002, p. 36.
90. According to data from the Bank for International Settlements, central bank interventions over the period from September 1992 to September 1993 amounted to at least $250 billion.
91. The story of Hungarian-American billionaire George Soros almost singlehandedly forcing the British pound out of the EMS has become legendary.
92. Schlesinger as quoted in the *Financial Times*, December 2, 1992.
93. De Silguy as quoted in Marsh, 2009, p. 184. Actually, de Silguy's warning was a veiled threat that France might take protectionist measures against devaluating countries like Spain and Portugal.
94. On the rather arbitrary character of these 3 percent and 60 percent limits, see Buiter et al., 1992.
95. All data are from the Economic Outlook of the OECD.
96. In May 1997, German Finance Minister Waigel proposed that the Bundesbank should revalue its stock of gold in accordance with market prices. Waigel wanted to use the proceeds of this revaluation to reduce the deficit of the government. Subtly mobilizing public opinion against this proposal, the Bundesbank succeeded in torpedoing the idea.
97. Mitterrand as quoted in Marsh, 2009, p. 187.
98. See for example the views expressed by former Bundesbank President Schlesinger in Schlesinger, 1996.
99. Issing as quoted in the German Weekly *Der Spiegel*, January 15, 1996. In Issing, 2002, he softened his argument on this issue considerably.
100. Tietmeyer as quoted in Marsh, 2009, p. 198.
101. Wilhelm Nölling was a former president of Hamburg's state central bank and a member of the Bundesbank Central Council.
102. Schmidt as quoted in *Spiegel Online*, June 30, 2010.
103. Schröder as quoted in *Bild Zeitung*, March 26, 1998.
104. As recounted in Marshall, 1999, p. 1–14.
105. In 1993, Duisenberg was asked to lead the EMI. Officially, he refused because his task as head of the Dutch central bank was still very demanding. In reality, Duisenberg refused because he thought at that time there was still too much uncertainty surrounding the EMU project.
106. Giscard d'Estaing as quoted in *Le Monde*, July 12, 1997.
107. See for example Eichengreen and Wyplosz, 1997. That conclusion would prove to be entirely correct.
108. Wyplosz in Baldwin, Gros, and Laeven, 2010, p. 34. In Wyplosz' analysis, the excessive deficit clause in the Maastricht Treaty led directly to the SGP.
109. Rocard as quoted in Marsh, 2009, p. 206.
110. See Trichet, 1992.
111. Helmut Hesse as quoted in *Le Monde*, November 6, 1997.
112. Tietmeyer in *The Independent* on April 26, 1998.
113. Blair, 2010.

114. Viktor Klima as referred to in the *International Herald Tribune*, May 4, 1998.
115. We refer especially to the March 1998 Convergence Reports of the European Commission and the European Monetary Institute.
116. Wellink as quoted in Marsh, 2009, p. 198.
117. Marsh, 2009, p. 207.
118. It was a nice sort of revenge for Duisenberg on Chirac that he held onto his job almost a year and a half longer than Chirac had openly claimed he would at the famous press conference in Brussels in early May of 1998.
119. Krugman, 2011.
120. For an excellent survey of the opinions of major American economists, see Jonung and Drea, 2009.
121. Friedman interviewed on May 2, 2000 and quoted in Samuelson and Barnett, 2007, p. 160.
122. Franco Modigliani interviewed on November 5, 1999 and quoted in Samuelson and Barnett, 2007, p. 104.
123. Dahrendorf in an article in the *New Statesman*, February 20, 1998.
124. Krugman, 2011.
125. For an in-depth review of the costs and benefits, see Alesina and Barro, 2002 and De Grauwe, 2003.
126. Giavazzi and Giovanini, 1989.
127. Nils Bernstein as quoted in the *Irish Independent*, October 1, 2009.
128. Helmut Kohl as quoted in the *Wall Street Journal Europe*, May 10, p. 6.
129. Davies and Green, 2010, p. 183.
130. Delors as quoted in Prior-Wandesforde and Hacche, 2005, p. 23.
131. Feldstein, 1997.
132. An asymmetric shock is a shock that hits the different members of the monetary union in different ways. For example: A drastic increase in the oil price will hit countries that import all their oil harder than it hits those who produce their own.
133. This argument obviously applies less for countries making serial devaluations a basic characteristic of their economic policy toolkit. One tends to think in this context especially about Italy in the post–World War II period.
134. We follow the discussion of OCA as outlined by Franceso Mongelli in Buti et al., 2010, p. 115-180.
135. Mundell, 1961.
136. Corden, 1972.
137. Fleming, 1971.
138. McKinnon, 1963.
139. Kenen, 1969.
140. Ingram, 1962.
141. Mundell, 1973.
142. Kenen, 1969.
143. Francesco Mongelli in Buti et al., 2010, p. 118. See also Mintz, 1970.
144. Haberler, 1970.
145. Mélitz, 1991.
146. Kirkegaard, 2010, p. 7.
147. Archer as quoted in Artis, 2002, p. 23.

148. For the history of monetary union in the U.S., see Friedman and Schwartz, 1963. For comparisons of the American experience with EMU, see Eichengreen, 1997, Bordo and Jonung, 2000 and Bordo, 2004.

149. Tilford, 2006, p. 11.

150. Krugman, 2011.

151. For an exploration of the long and sometimes painful road to fiscal federalism in the United States, see Rodden, 2006.

152. Sala-i-Martin and Sachs, 1992.

153. Kim, 1998 and Margo, 1998.

154. European Commission, 2002.

155. OECD, 1999. See also Molloy, Smith, and Wozniak, 2011.

156. Krugman, "Lessons of Massachusetts for EMU" in Torres and Giavazzi, 1993.

157. Duisenberg as quoted in Lynn, p. 30.

158. Brown, 2010, p. 186.

159. It was not unusual for OCA theory to be totally absent in discussions about the economics of the euro area. A typical but by no means unique example of this neglect would be Van Bergeijk, Berndsen, and Jansen, 2000.

160. Speech by Trichet at the Land Central Bank of Rheinland-Palatinate and the Saarland, Mainz, Germany, June 2, 1997.

161. Marsh, 2009, p. 103.

162. See Robson, 1987. For an argument to the contrary, see for example Artis, 2002.

163. Tavlas, 1993 and 1994.

164. See Tavlas, 1994 for more on this inconsistency issue.

165. Emerson et al., 1992.

166. Willem Buiter referred to this finding as the "fine-tuning fallacy." See Buiter, 1999.

167. For more on this issue, see for example, Calvo and Reinhart, 2000.

168. See for example Frankel and Rose, 1996 and 1997.

169. Kenen, 1969 and Eichengreen, 1992.

170. Frankel and Rose, 1996, p. 2,3.

171. Krugman and Venables, 1996.

172. De Grauwe and Mongelli, 2005, p. 29.

173. See Chapter 1: The Maastricht Mantra for the convergence criteria as laid down in the Maastricht Treaty.

174. Ubide in Baldwin, Gros, and Laeven, eds., 2010, p. 45.

175. De Bandt and Mongelli, 2000.

176. Padoa-Schioppa, 2000.

177. Corden, 2002.

178. Lachman, 2010, p. 11.

179. Wyplosz in Baldwin, Gros, and Laeven, eds., 2010, p. 34, 35.

180. Burda and Gerlach in Baldwin, Gros, and Laeven, eds., 2010, p. 65, 66.

181. Jonung, 2010.

182. OECD, 2000.

183. See Duval and Elmeskov, 2006.

184. Alesina, Ardagna, and Galasso, 2010, in Alesina and Giavazzi, eds., p. 59.

185. Smigiel, 2010, p. 38.

186. André Saphir brought the importance of this argument to my attention.

187. See Jacobi and Kluve, 2006 for a description of the Hartz reforms and a first evaluation of their effects.
188. The German electorate did not share that opinion. In 2005 the coalition of socialists and *die Grünen* was beaten, ending the chancellorship of Gerhard Schröder.
189. Buti et al., 2010, p. 9.
190. Benjamin Cohen in Dyson, 2008, p. 38.
191. De Grauwe, 2003, p. 174.
192. For critical reviews of the Lisbon Aganda, see Kok Group, 2004 and Wyplosz, 2010.
193. Tilford and Whyte, 2010, p. 3.
194. Steinbrück as quoted in Marsh, 2009, p. 219.
195. European Commission, 2008.
196. Issing in Goldman Sachs, 2008, p.17.
197. Buti et al., 2010, p. xxvii.
198. Speech by Trichet made in Osnabruck, Germany on February 12, 2009. Available on the website of the ECB.
199. Mandelson as quoted in *Mail Online*, June 12, 2009.
200. Goldman Sachs, 2008, p. 12.
201. Tilford, 2009, p.1–2.
202. Tilford, 2006, p. 1, 57, 58.
203. Lawson as quoted in Marsh, 2009, p. 247.
204. Bootle, 2009, p. 20.
205. The German weekly *Der Spiegel* revealed the extent of Goldman Sachs' involvement in Greece's attempt to fudge its numbers. See "How Goldman Sachs Helped Greece to Mask its True Debt," *Der Spiegel*, February 28, 2010.
206. At the end of 2010, Willem Buiter and Ebrahim Rahbari composed a list of the advanced countries whose public finances were still in a reasonable shape: Australia, New Zealand, Denmark, Norway, Sweden, Finland, and Switzerland. Finland is the only member of the eurozone on this list. See Buiter and Rahbari, 2010.
207. Papantoniou as quoted in *World News*, August 23, 1999.
208. Buiter and Sibert, 2006.
209. Lynn, 2011, p. 53.
210. Bini Smaghi, 2011a, p. 2.
211. The *Economist*, November 20, 2010.
212. This argument needs some nuancing since, especially in Ireland, government receipts depended to a considerable extent on receipts related to the bubble-like growth in the construction and real estate sector.
213. Avinash Persaud in Baldwin, Gros, and Laeven, eds., 2010, p. 56.
214. Tilford and Whyte, 2010.
215. Daniel Gros, "Financial Stability: 'Collective Leadership' will not work," *CEPS Commentary*, March 9, 2011.
216. Reluctance to have the IMF involved in the euro crisis was initially high, especially at the ECB.
217. A country in Greece's position could gain from a devaluation of the euro vis-à-vis, for example, the dollar and the yen. But that would not, of course, improve Greece's competitive position *inside* the EMU.
218. *The Economist* referred to the "fiendish complexity" of the proposals. See Charlemagne's Notebook, May 10, 2010.

219. See Rahbari, Michels, and Giani, 2011, p. 29.
220. Two insiders to that weekend's discussions revealed off the record to the author the extreme sharpness of the discussions.
221. According to the Spanish newspaper *El Pais*, Spanish prime minister José Luis Zapatero claimed that during the weekend of May 8 and 9, 2010, when the euro crisis was at its high point, Sarkozy "beat his fist on the table and threatened to withdraw from the euro." (As reported in the *Financial Times*, May 17, 2010.) As far as we know, there's no official record of this threat making any impression on Merkel and her closest advisors.
222. Chapter 4 more extensively examines the German issue.
223. De Mazière as quoted in *The Economist*, Charlemagne's Notebook, May 20, 2010.
224. It was later revealed that four other members of the ECB's governing council privately also opposed the SMP step.
225. Weber as quoted on Bloomberg, May 10, 2010.
226. *Frankfurter Allgemeine Zeitung*, May 10, 2010.
227. Their action was briefly described in Chapter 1: To delay or not.
228. Their complaint would again be rejected by the court.
229. *The Economist*, December 2, 2010. See also Chapter 4 on the German opposition to monetary union and the euro.
230. Weber, 2010, p. 2.
231. Trichet as quoted on guardian.co.uk, December 2, 2010.
232. Krugman in the *International Herald Tribune*, November 30, 2010.
233. The BIS publishes quarterly International Banking Statistics. Tables 9A to D contain aggregated data on the international exposure of banks.
234. The CEBS had about thirty employees at the time of the stress tests, compared with more than three thousand at the UK financial regulator, the Financial Services Authority.
235. In private conversations with several economists working at the ECB, similar numbers popped up.
236. Zeitler as quoted in the *New York Times*, July 23, 2010 and Schäuble in *dw-world.de*, July 24, 2010.
237. Rogoff as quoted in *Midas Letter*, December, 9, 2010.
238. Annunziata as quoted in the *New York Times*, July, 23, 2010.
239. Hahn as quoted in *Midas Letter*, December 9, 2010.
240. Véron as quoted in *Midas Letter*, December 9, 2010.
241. For a much more positive evaluation of the stress tests, see Lannoo, 2010.
242. See for example the reporting in the *Wall Street Journal* of September 7, 2010.
243. Gary Jenkins, head of fixed income at Evolution Securities, as quoted in the *Financial Times*, November 29, 2010.
244. *The Economist*, November 20, 2010.
245. Barroso as quoted on the Brussels blog of the *Financial Times*, October 28, 2010.
246. See the information on guardian.co.uk, October 29, 2010.
247. Papandreou as quoted in the *Financial Times*, November 16, 2010.
248. Van Rompuy as quoted on euobserver.com, November 16, 2010.
249. *Financial Times*, November 16 and November 19, 2010.
250. *Financial Times*, January 14, 2011.
251. *Financial Times*, November 19, 2010.

252. Lenihan as quoted in the *Financial Times*, November 22, 2010.

253. Regling as quoted in Buiter, Rahbari, Michels, and Giani, 2011, p. 35.

254. To illustrate the difference between Spain and the smaller countries such as Greece, Ireland, and Portugal, it was calculated that Portugal needed 51.5 billion euros over the next three years to cover its expected budget deficits and the repayment of maturing bonds. The equivalent amount for Spain is 350 billion euros. Calculations by HSBC as reported in the *Wall Street Journal*, November 23, 2010.

255. Salgado and Sócrates as quoted in the *Financial Times*, November 23, 2010.

256. Van Rompuy as quoted in the *International Herald Tribune*, November 24, 2010.

257. Merkel as quoted in the *Wall Street Journal*, November 24, 2010.

258. Schäuble as quoted in the *Financial Times*, December 6, 2010.

259. Parker as quoted in the *Financial Times*, November 30, 2010.

260. *Financial Times*, November 26, 2010.

261. *The Economist*, November 20, 2010.

262. Issing in the *Financial Times*, December 2, 2010.

263. See the reports in the *Financial Times* and *Wall Street Journal*.

264. Martin Wolf in the *Financial Times*, December 1, 2010.

265. Report as quoted in the *International Herald Tribune*, December 1, 2010.

266. As reported in the *Financial Times*, December 4, 2010.

267. Juncker and Tremonti in an op-ed piece in the *Financial Times*, December 6, 2010. See also the *Wall Street Journal*, December 7, 2010.

268. Strauss-Kahn as quoted in the *Financial Times*, December 8, 2010.

269. Report quoted in the *Wall Street Journal*, December 17, 2010.

270. *Wall Street Journal*, December 29, 2010.

271. *Financial Times*, December 20, 2010.

272. As reported in the *Financial Times*, December 18, 2010.

273. *International Herald Tribune*, January 6, 2011.

274. Issing, 2011, p. 13

275. Sócrates in the *Financial Times*, January 12, 2011.

276. Salgado as quoted in the *Wall Street Journal*, January 11, 2011.

277. *Financial Times*, January 12, 2011.

278. Schäuble as quoted in the *Financial Times*, January 14, 2011.

279. *Wall Street Journal*, January 12, 2011.

280. *Financial Times*, January 25, 2011. That 8 percent is more than the 7 percent ratio required to be satisfied by 2019 under the Basel III capital adequacy ratios.

281. See reporting in the *Financial Times*, June 10, 2011.

282. See for example the reporting in the *Wall Street Journal*, May 20, 2011.

283. Vazquez as quoted in the *International Herald Tribune*, January 28, 2011.

284. Sarkozy as quoted in the *Financial Times*, January 28, 2011.

285. Lagarde and Schäuble as quoted in the *Financial Times*, January 31, 2011.

286. Remark made off the record to the author.

287. Summers as quoted in the *Financial Times*, January 28, 2011.

288. Lipsky as quoted in the *Financial Times*, January 31, 2011.

289. See for example the contribution of Takis Michas to the *Wall Street Journal*, April 13, 2011, under the title "Greece's Rule of Lawlessness."

290. How, when, and by whom the details of this plan were hammered out was described in the *International Herald Tribune*, March 3, 2011 and in the *Wall Street Journal*, April 14, 2011.

291. Stelzer in the *Wall Street Journal*, February 7, 2011.

292. Leterme as quoted in the *Wall Street Journal*, February 7, 2011.

293. A diplomat quoted Polish Prime Minister Donald Tusk as challenging Merkel and Sarkozy aggressively by asking: "Do you really think you have the right to treat all the others this way?" (*International Herald Tribune*, February 22, 2011).

294. Buiter as quoted in the *International Herald Tribune*, January 12, 2011.

295. *Financial Times*, February 7, 2011.

296. A major problem for all these publicly owned regional banks is that a large part of their capital base consists of their so-called silent participations, which are sums borrowed from state governments. Dieter Posch, the economics minister of the German state of Hesse, called upon the state-owned Landesbank Hessen-Thüeringen to boycott new European bank stress tests.

297. Franz as quoted in the *International Herald Tribune*, February 15, 2011.

298. See Haufler et al., 2011.

299. Trichet, 2011a.

300. *Financial Times*, March 11, 2011.

301. The wildly differing estimates of the recapitalization needs of Spanish banks were highly illustrative of the lack of solid and credible information on the true state of the European banking sector.

302. *Financial Times*, March 14, 2011.

303. Ferguson as quoted in the *Wall Street Journal*, March 14, 2011.

304. *Financial Times*, March 14, 2011.

305. In the case of a default by, again for example, Greece, private investors were supposed to take the major hit, not the countries guaranteeing the EFSF credits. The first of these was Germany (certainly in the not-so-theoretical case that France, given its budget deficit and level of government, would also lose its AAA rating).

306. Daniel Gros in *CEPS Commentary*, "Tough Talk but Soft Conditions?" March 16, 2011.

307. Juncker as quoted in the *International Herald Tribune*, March 25, 2011.

308. Tilford as quoted in the *International Herald Tribune*, April 11, 2011.

309. *Financial Times*, April 9, 2011. Two anonymous sources inside the ECB confirmed to the author the pressure that had been exercised on the Portuguese banks.

310. *Financial Times*, April 8, 2011.

311. See section titled "Turning to Lisbon, Eyeing Madrid."

312. *Financial Times*, April 8, 2011.

313. Salgado as quoted in the *Wall Street Journal*, April 18, 2011.

314. Vinals as quoted in the *Financial Times*, April 14, 2011.

315. Münchau as quoted in the *Financial Times*, April 11, 2011.

316. *Financial Times*, April 15, 2011.

317. The ECB also found it increasingly difficult to sterilize the inflationary potential of its bond-buying program.

318. Data available on the ECB's website. Irish banks alone absorbed 180 of the 550 billion euros.

319. *Financial Times*, May 3, 2011. The leader of the True Finns elaborated on his views on the euro situation in a contribution to the *Wall Street Journal*, May 9, 2011.

320. Moody's had put U.S. debt on negative outlook in 1996.

321. Schäuble as quoted in the *Financial Times*, April 27, 2011.

322. *Financial Times*, May 12, 2011.

323. Interest payments on government debt stood at 5.6 percent of GDP.

324. Already in February 2011 the IMF warned that the Greek program "remains at a crossroads." The *Financial Times* reported that officials involved in the Greek program called such a description "a massive understatement" (*Financial Times*, May 2, 2011).

325. According to a banker anonymously quoted by the *Financial Times*, April 16, 2011.

326. *Wall Street Journal*, April 15, 2011.

327. Hoyer as quoted in the *Financial Times*, April 16, 2011.

328. Rehn as quoted in the *Financial Times*, April 18, 2011.

329. "Greece Considers Exit from Euro Zone," *Spiegel Online*, May 5, 2011

330. Blejer in the *Financial Times*, May 6, 2011.

331. Juncker as quoted in the *Financial Times*, May 9, 2011.

332. Juncker and Rehn as quoted in the *Financial Times*, May 18, 2011.

333. A CDS is basically an insurance contract where one party pays an annual premium to protect itself against the default of a bond issuer. The determination of whether a restructuring would be counted as a payout triggering event is determined by a panel of dealers and buyers from the International Swaps and Derivatives Association (ISDA). *The Economist* reported in its June 2, 2011 issue that under ISDA rules each region has a "determination committee," made up of ten bankers and five investors, that rules on such issues. Any market participant can ask for a ruling. Unless it is backed by a super-majority of twelve out of fifteen members, the decision is passed to an external review committee of independent experts, a kind of supreme court for the CDS market.

334. *The Economist*, June 2, 2011.

335. See for example the reporting in the *Financial Times* of May 19 and 20, 2011. Early in May, ECB president Jean-Claude Trichet had already furiously walked out of a meeting of finance ministers when the possibility of Greek debt restructuring was raised. For an elaborated version of the ECB's arguments, see Bini Smaghi, 2011(b).

336. Stark as quoted in the *Wall Street Journal*, May 20, 2011. Shortly afterward, Christian Noyer, the governor of the Bank of France, repeated Stark's threat. See the *Wall Street Journal*, May 26, 2011.

337. *Financial Times*, May 23, 2011.

338. *Wall Street Journal*, May 27, 2011.

339. Sfakianakis in the *Financial Times*, June 9, 2011.

340. Damanaki as quoted on the website of the London-based think tank Open Europe, May 26, 2011.

341. Vermeend in *De Telegraaf*, May 31, 2011.

342. Joffe in the *Wall Street Journal*, May 31, 2011.

343. Schäuble as quoted in the *Financial Times Deutschland*, May 30, 2011.

344. Schäffler as quoted on the website of Open Europe, June 9, 2011.

345. *Financial Times*, June 1, 2011.

346. *The Economist*, June 11, 2011, p. 33.

347. Wellink in the *Financial Times*, June 16, 2011.
348. Brittan in the *Financial Times*, June 24, 2011.
349. Cochrane and Kashyap in the *Wall Street Journal*, June 17, 2011.
350. Gérard Lafay, Jacques Sapir, and Philippe Villina in the French daily *Le Figaro*, June 22, 2011.
351. Münchau in *Prospect*, July 2011, p. 28.
352. Position paper of the European Commission quoted in the *Financial Times*, July 5, 2011.
353. Tremonti as quoted in *Financial Times Deutschland*, July 9, 2011.
354. Schäuble as quoted in *Financial Times Deutshland*, July 14, 2011.
355. *Börsen Zeitung*, July 19, 2011.
356. Quotes taken from the *Financial Times*.
357. Weidmann as quoted in the *Financial Times*, July 23, 2011.
358. Lauk as quoted in the *Financial Times*, July 25, 2011.
359. As quoted in the *Wall Street Journal*, July 25, 2011.
360. *Financial Times*, August 6, 2011.
361. Barroso as quoted in the *Financial Times*, August 4, 2011.
362. Otmar Issing in the *Financial Times*, August 9, 2011.
363. Dyson, 2008, p. 9.
364. Counting the engagement of the IMF, the stabilization fund amounts to 750 billion euros.
365. See the contribution of Takis Michas to the *Wall Street Journal*, April 13, 2011 and the one of John Sfakianakis to the *Financial Times*, June 9, 2011.
366. Münchau in the *Financial Times*, April 25, 2011.
367. Buiter and Rahbari, 2010, p. 10.
368. See the discussion in Chapter 3: Bogus Tests Fuel Stress.
369. We leave aside here the alphabet soup of different mechanisms (EFSF, ESM, EFSM, etc.) that have been set up in the course of the crisis.
370. See for example the contribution of Nicholas Spiro on the risks for Germany to the *Wall Street Journal*, March 29, 2011.
371. *The Economist*, June 11, 2011.
372. See Chapter 3: Keep on Ponzi Scheming.
373. A typical opinion on the conundrum policymakers in countries such as Germany had maneuvered themselves into was vented by Ranier Hank, the senior economics editor of Germany's most serious newspaper, *Frankfurter Allgemeine Zeitung*: "Saving Greece is not a useful thing to do. It damages us" (*FAZ*, June 13, 2011).
374. Tilford, 2011.
375. Data taken from the OECD Economic Outlook.
376. Data taken from OECD, Economic Outlook, May 2011.
377. Based on the data for 2010 available in the Statistics Pocket Book of the ECB, April 2011.
378. Paul Krugman in the *International Herald Tribune*, November 30, 2011.
379. There is a real prospect of a breakup of Belgium into a Dutch-speaking, more conservative Flemish part and a French-speaking, more socialist Walloon part at the time of finalization of this book (end of August 2011).
380. Data from the OECD Economic Outlook.

381. Intergenerational accounting tries to discover where government debt goes if present policies are left unchanged. Leading experts on this technique are Larry Kotlikoff of Boston University and Jagadeesh Gokhale of the Cato Institute. For more on the situation of France in this context, see Gokhale, 2009.

382. Kashyap, Schoenholtz, and Hyun Song Shin in the *Wall Street Journal*, March 23, 2011. See also in this respect Greenlaw *et al.*, 2011.

383. Lamont as quoted in the *International Herald Tribune*, December 29, 2010.

384. An interesting argument has been made by Panicos Demetriades of the Department of Economics at the University of Leicester (UK). Demetriades argues that it is Germany that should leave the eurozone, not the peripheral countries in distress. The euro without Germany would depreciate considerably and restore overnight the distressed countries' international competitiveness. Demetriades made these remarks in a letter to the *Financial Times*, May 19, 2011.

385. The discussion of the Argentinian experience is based on the contribution of Uri Dadush and Bennett Stancil in Dadush, 2010; Nechio, 2010; and on the IMF reports on Argentina.

386. Dadush and Stancil in Dadush, 2010, p. 33–34.

387. See the comparison between the two countries in Nechio, 2010.

388. Important to realize when making the comparison between both countries is that the currency mismatch in the balance sheets of the national banking system was much worse in Argentina than it is in Greece. More than 90 percent of assets and liabilities of Greek bonds are denominated in euros, so a currency replacement would not fundamentally destabilize the banks' balance sheets.

389. Flanagan as quoted in the *IMF Survey Magazine*, October 5, 2010.

390. To give an idea of the order of magnitudes: In Ireland, a country that also suffered from a huge banking crisis, the ratio of bank assets to GDP grew to a factor of three.

391. This standby agreement contained a credit line for Iceland of 2.2 billion dollars, a sum equal to 20 percent of the country's GDP. Iceland was also granted important bridging loans by countries from Nordic Europe.

392. Asgeir Jonsson in the *Wall Street Journal*, June 16, 2011. See also Jonsson, 2009.

393. For more details on the policies and their evaluation by the IMF, see the IMF's country report on Iceland (no. 11/125, June 2011).

394. This approach led to major disagreements with foreign governments, especially the British and Dutch, on the internet bank Icesave that by the summer of 2011 still were far from settled.

395. Sigfusson as quoted in *The Economist*, April 16, 2011.

396. As reported in the *Financial Times*, January 27, 2007.

397. According to an opinion poll carried out by Allensbach, 63 percent of Germans have little or no confidence in the EU. To 53 percent of Germans, Europe is no longer the future (as reported by the *Frankfurter Allgemeine Zeitung*, January 25, 2011).

398. Juncker as quoted in Marsh, 2009, p. 242.

399. See for example several of the contributions in Baldwin, Gros, and Laeven, 2010. For earlier proposals in this respect, see Fatas, *et al*, 2003.

400. Tilford, 2010b, p. 2.

401. Tietmeyer as quoted in Marsh, 2009, p. 194.

402. Also hard to ignore in this context is the fact that national politicians have "misused" Europe. Whenever unpopular measures (e.g., cutting public services, reducing wage costs, increasing taxes) needed to be taken, politicians stumbled over each other to blame Europe. This behavior fed public displeasure with Europe.

403. See Chapter 3: Grand Bargain Turning Surreal.

404. Ubide in Baldwin, Gros, and Laeven, 2010, p. 47.

405. Barroso in *Frankfurter Allgemeine Zeitung*, May 25, 2010.

406. Guérot and Leonard, 2011, p. 1.

407. *Financial Times*, April 12, 2011.

408. Merkel in her 2011 New Year's speech as quoted in the *Wall Street Journal*, January 5, 2011.

409. Merkel as quoted in the *International Herald Tribune*, May 25, 2011.

410. Rachman in the *Financial Times*, November 29, 2010.

411. Martin Wolf in the *Financial Times*, December 1, 2010.

412. Buiter and Rahbari, 2010, p. 11.

413. Schröder as quoted in Marsh, 2009, p. 221.

414. Ruling of the Constitutional Court as reprinted in Proissl, 2010, p. 15.

415. See Chapter 3: Weber's Infighting.

416. Bérégovoy as quoted in Aeschimann and Riché, 1996, p. 137.

417. Mitterrand and Chirac as quoted in Proissl, 2010, p. 11.

418. Guérot and Leonard, 2011, p. 5.

419. Barber in the *Financial Times*, April 18, 2011.

420. Based on Eurostat data.

421. Bastian in the *Financial Times*, January 17, 2011.

422. Guérot and Leonard, 2011, p. 5.

423. Henkel, 2010.

424. See interview with Spethmann in FAZ.NET, February 7, 2011.

425. Guérot and Leonard, 2011, p. 3.

426. Schmidt as quoted in Marsh, 2009, p. 84.

427. Schimdt in the German weekly *Die Zeit*, August 6, 1993.

428. Kirkegaard, 2010, p. 8.

429. Kimmitt as quoted in Marsh, 2009, p. 103.

430. Proissl, 2010, p. 4.

431. The remainder of this paragraph is taken from Guérot and Leonard, 2011, p. 7.

432. *Die Zeit*, July 29, 2010, p. 7.

433. De Mazière as quoted in *The Economist*, Charlemagne's Notebook, May 20, 2010.

434. Barysch, 2010, p. 3.

435. Mitterrand as quoted in Marsh, 2009, p. 93.

436. *The Economist*, Charlemagne's Notebook, May 20, 2010.

437. Proissl, 2010, p. 3.

438. Mitterrand as quoted in Marsh, 2009, p. 139.

439. Schröder as quoted in Marsh, 2009, p. 221.

440. Guérot and Leonard, 2011, p. 2.

441. Guérot and Leonard, 2011, p. 3.

442. Proissl, 2010, p. 24.

443. For more on this complicated relationship, see for example Hoffmann, 1995. Also informative is the lead article "The Odd Couple at Europe's Helm" in the *International Herald Tribune*, January 15, 2011.
444. Prodi as quoted in Guérot and Leonard, 2011, p. 4.
445. Lagarde as quoted in the *International Herald Tribune*, January 20, 2011.
446. Lorenzi, 2011, p. 9.
447. Mitterrand as quoted in Marsh, 2009, p. 139.
448. Lorenzi, 2011, p. 9, 10.
449. Proissl, 2010, p. 5.
450. Dobrindt as quoted in the *Frankfurter Allgemeine Zeitung*, June 6, 2011.
451. Barysch, 2010, p. 2, 3.
452. Adams as quoted in the *Wall Street Journal*, December 6, 2010.
453. Cohen in the *International Herald Tribune*, November 11, 2010.

Index